PARENTING THROUGH THE FOUR SEASONS

PARENTING
THROUGH
THE FOUR SEASONS

Chanty Webb

Parenting Through The Four Seasons

Printed in the USA ISBN 978-1-941173-42-8

Published by

Olive **P**ress Messianic and Christian Publisher
www.olivepresspublisher.com
olivepressbooks@gmail.com

Our prayer at Olive Press is that we may help make the Word of Adonai fully known, that it spread rapidly and be glorified everywhere. We hope our books help open people's eyes so they will turn from darkness to Light and from the power of the adversary to God and to trust in ישוע Yeshua (Jesus). (From II Thess. 3:1; Col. 1:25; Acts 26:18,15 NRSV and CJB) .

Front cover photographs: Lifetouch, JCPenney Portraits.

Back cover photograph: Lisa Q Shay Photography

In honor to God, pronouns referring to the Trinity are capitalized. But not all Bible versions do this and legally must be printed as they are.

For My Four Seasons: Morgan, Hunter, Blaise, and Story

CONTENTS

Preface

Can you identify with this scenario? You're in your home. The kids are occupied. All is quiet (did I lose you already?). You think to yourself, *This is the perfect time to return that phone call I received earlier today.* You pick up the phone, dial the number, and as soon as the words, "Hello this is..." escape your mouth, chaos erupts. Sister hits brother. Baby wants a bottle. Teenager Mike is begging for the car keys and Tweener Twila begins practicing drums. This craziness could have broken out any other time of day. WHY *NOW?!*

The above scenario sums up my current state of mind. I just completed a final read through of my manuscript, am on the verge of sending it to my publisher and wouldn't you know it—the kids decide to act up.

Don't get me wrong. They've acted up before. But right now? Now when I'm about to send off my parenting book to be published, there is some pretty significant kid drama goin' down in the Webb household.

Initially my mind was trying to reason how I could be qualified to promote a parenting book at a time when my kids are struggling in life. But then the thought came to me: who better to hear from? Would you rather get guidance from a parent who has never been jarred by the actions of her child? Or someone seasoned by withstanding the storms that come with the poor choices and missed opportunities of her beloved brood?

In the pages that follow, I give you exactly what I want from a fellow parent: transparency, honesty, integrity, hope. But the only reason I have these qualities to give is because of Jesus living in me.

Jesus has given me peace even in this time when blow after devastating blow has hit me through my children. This same peace is for you as well because Jesus made a way for every person to have relationship with Him. If you confess with your mouth that Jesus is Lord and believe in your heart that God raised Him from the dead, **you will be saved**.

My prayer is that you choose to accept the peace that God gives through accepting His Son Jesus Christ as Lord and Savior of your life. Making this decision entitles you to be raised by the best Parent ever!

Introduction

Four kids. Four seasons.

Morgan age 21 born in the spring. Hunter age 20 born in the summer. Blaise age 16 born in the winter. Story age 7 born in the fall.

I call them my Four Seasons.

In raising them, my husband Ross and I have observed the various stages of childhood equal to their number: preschool, school age, tween, and teen. Ecclesiastes 3:1 tells us that for everything there is a season, and a time for every matter under heaven.

A time to plant, and a time to uproot

A time to tear down and a time to build

A time to weep and a time to laugh

A time to keep and a time to throw away

A time to be silent and a time to speak

Continuing in those first verses of chapter three reveals even more dichotomy of the parenting experience—some joy-filled, others heart-breaking. Yet one central theme ties them together—seasons.

Living in Pennsylvania I get to experience all four seasons. Quite honestly, I don't like it. I would much rather see green plant life and soak in the sun all year round. Yet one of the most satisfying sights for me is seeing those first few flowers come up in early spring. Despite the fact that temperatures are still fluctuating and occasionally dip down to freezing overnight, the daffodil and tulip bulbs faithfully send up their first green leaf. Upon seeing this sight my soul fills with delight. Why? Because I know there is more to come. You see, after that one leaf will be another, and then a stem, and eventually what I waited so patiently for all winter long will emerge—a breath-taking blossom.

Such is parenting. Our winter is the stress, strain, and strife that comes with leading our kids in the way they should go. But as we put in the work and wait patiently, we soon see what we have been waiting for all along— growth. By God's grace we see those faithful green leaves even in contrary conditions.

Perhaps your conditions are different than mine. Maybe you are raising a grandchild. Or maybe you are a single father faithfully doing hair and serving on the PTO. Or maybe you're one of the superheroes known as foster parents with the power to love kids needing to be rescued. We may not share the same circumstances, but if you are reading this book, we do share the same concern— growing the children under our care into capable adults who know their worth in this world.

Our kids keep us learning. As experiences, anxieties, and expectations come into their lives, we seek out wisdom to help them through. One would assume that it gets easier with each child. I say it only gets *different* with each child. Due to these differences, I remain a student of parenting God's way.

This book is not to tell you how to raise your kids, but to share with you how we are raising our own—Morgan, Hunter, Blaise, and Story—the Four Seasons.

Chapter 1

FIRST COMES LOVE

"A baseball team"

That's the response I got from my husband whenever I asked him how many children he would like us to have. We were still dating at the time, so in his defense I had every opportunity to jump ship right there and then. If it weren't for those gorgeous blue eyes of his…

I would laugh it off whenever he mentioned it. My vision of us as a married couple was footloose and fancy-free traveling on a whim with no commitments. I was never a "kid" person. Some women *love* to babysit or just *have* to hold a baby. Not me. I had no interest at all.

Well, Ross and I got married in August of 1999 and found out we were pregnant about one month later. Classic honeymoon baby. I am a woman and a nurse. I realize that when you don't take measures to prevent becoming pregnant, chances are you become pregnant. But somehow, I was still overcome by the shock of it all. My expectations were to spend our first year of marriage settling into our nest. Instead we began planning to add a little chick to our nest.

Two weeks prior to having our daughter, we moved from an apartment into a home. Having a home gave us more space, but more importantly, it provided privacy for us as a couple. Through our church, we had superb teaching on married life, both formally and through examples lived out before us. One teaching that we were both committed to was putting our marriage relationship before our children. Hebrews 13:4 says, "Marriage should be honored by all, and the marriage bed kept pure…" One way our children can honor our marriage is by giving us privacy, and when they are too little to do that on their own, we do it for them by letting them sleep in their own room.

It has been over 20 years since we had our first child, so I don't recollect all of my emotions surrounding keeping Morgan in a separate room. I do however recall attending to the baby monitor as if I were a bookie listening to a horse race on the radio. Ross on the other hand did not have any difficulty leaving our daughter in her own room. He lavished in being able to have his still-new bride all to himself at night. Although it was more challenging for me, I'm glad we stayed committed to this practice and made each other a priority over our first-born child.

For the sake of honesty, I must share that Story, our youngest son, did get to cohabitate with us for about 6 months. This was purely for logistical purposes. You see, we lived in a three-bedroom home. So right up until the time he was born we were undecided as to how to handle our living arrangements with now four children. We didn't find out his gender ahead of time and had been thinking, *Since we have two boys already sharing one room, if it's a girl, she can just move into the room with Morgan.* When my neighbor who delivered Story (a story that I'll share later) exclaimed, "It's a boy!" I was in disbelief. What now? We had no plans for if "It's a boy."

We knew that we could not put him in the boys' room right off the bat because his sleeping was inconsistent at night. Compromising their sleep would not be a good commercial for moving him into their room in the future. So, we decided to keep him in our room until he was past the stage of waking up in the middle of the night. I remember Ross regularly asking me when we were going to move him out of our room. Like I said, my husband was ready to have our privacy back. I was ready too, but also reluctant. I worried about his older brother putting things into his crib that were not suitable for him. I also worried if he would not sleep as well because of the boys coming into the room later to go to sleep and rising early to get ready for school. I'll admit my Mommy antennae were going haywire.

Then there was the issue of space. Looking at the boys' room I did not see how a crib could even fit in there. They shared a bunk bed and had a dresser of drawers which left them with little room to spare. I hated the idea of taking any extra square footage away from them. Regardless, one day I took Hunter swimming with a friend and when I returned the crib was nearly fully assembled in their room. The best part about it was the room didn't look as cramped as I had expected. There was still a significant amount of open area even with the additional piece of furniture. I am thankful to my husband for moving ahead with keeping our commitment when I was wavering.

For all of our children, giving Mom and Dad privacy manifests itself in many ways. It could be knocking on the door and waiting to be invited inside of our bedroom or not coming into a room in which we are having a private conversation. As much as we instill respect for our privacy within our children, we are also intentional in demonstrating affection in their presence. Friends of ours used to call us "the couple who always kisses." Not a bad reputation to have.

Even today whenever we come to or leave one another, we give each other a kiss. It could be at a parent-teacher conference that we arrive at individually, or when Ross enters the door from work. During reach out time at church, we turn to each other first and greet one another with a hug and a kiss, to which those congregants around us inevitably tease, "Go get a room!" I can specifically remember a time when I was within earshot of a married woman who had just received a hug and exclaimed, "I needed that. I haven't had a hug all day." I cannot relate. Ross is the one who drives the affection. I am not a touchy person, but touch is a big need for him. I love how God has fashioned him with this characteristic and how He uses it as a witnessing tool for Christ both outside and inside our home.

Our children are no strangers to seeing a passionate embrace in the middle of the kitchen. Sometimes they show pretend disgust, whereas other times they join in on the affection by wrapping their arms around us both.

To be very transparent, when our oldest son, Hunter, used to empty the trash, for quite a few years, we had intentionally wrapped up our condom wrappers before placing them in the bedroom trash. Well, one day when he was older, we decided to stop hiding them. I can remember the first time he saw one. He gave us this big, long stare with raised eyebrows which clearly said, "You two? That's gross!" I teased him about being so unfortunate as to have parents that are attracted to each other. After encountering this visual numerous times, the shock of it all disappeared and I began to imagine him saying in his mind, "Mom and Dad had sex again," then just moving on to the next trashcan.

In putting one another first, we can demonstrate to our children what it looks like to put God first. As a matter of fact, the Bible speaks of the marriage relationship being like Christ's relationship with us, His church. Ephesians 5 paints a picture of how a husband and wife are to relate with one another. Then it shares that this relating should mirror how Christ and believers relate. As a child sees Mommy respect Daddy with her words and sees Daddy loving Mommy with his actions, she gets a firsthand account of the responsibilities of a believer in Jesus.

When we first got married, we lived on the bottom floor of a home rented out as apartments. The couple next to us had a young son who was about four or five years old. What I remember most about this family is that their preschooler ruled the roost. He lacked self-discipline and although his parents were nice people, they did not train him in the way he should go. As a result, he was still sleeping in their bed with no immediate plans in place to move him into his own room. I can remember having conversations to try and offer counsel (keep in mind we were only expecting our first child at the time), but it would always come down to them defending his behaviors. Certainly, the bedroom is not the only place where limits should be set for children, but it's a very important place to start. Why?

A husband and wife's bedroom is where sexual intimacy occurs. Sex is a gift from God to a man and his wife, designed by God for them to enjoy. They have exclusive permission to come together in this way only with one another. It is a very special, very powerful act.

When anything or anyone intrudes upon this act, it is not within God's design. The same freedom with just the two of them no longer exists. Remember when the serpent (Satan) came up to talk to Eve about eating of the fruit from the tree of good and evil (Genesis 3). After he entered the picture, Adam and Eve were embarrassed that they were naked. Before this, they were perfectly content and free to walk around exposed. Similarly, allowing a child to sleep with mommy and daddy takes away the liberty couples have in the sex act.

How long do we have before he wakes up?
Shhh, don't wake the baby!
I'm not comfortable doing "it" when she's in the room with us.

Hence, division results. Man and wife cannot experience the "one flesh" mentality talked about in Genesis 2. So then, if, in this very intimate, sacred part of the marriage relationship, a child is permitted to rule, it easily paves the way for them ruling in other areas.

In yet another Biblical example, Rebekah let her love for her son, Jacob, take precedence over her relationship with her husband, Isaac (Genesis 27). Not only did she premeditate deceiving her husband to get a blessing for this youngest son, she also actively engaged her beloved son in the deception. Rebekah wasn't alone in playing favorites. The Bible tells us that Jacob favored Esau. But it does not state that his favoritism caused him to sin. Rebekah put herself into a position that separated the two (she and her husband) that God had made one.

After living on this earth for over 40 years and living in Christ over 20 years, it has become plainly clear to me that God knows what He is doing. The way He has designed things is for our good and for His glory. Now, does He need to do things for our good? Absolutely not. What right do we have to be happy or to have peace? None. It is only because of His loving grace and His sustaining mercy that we have any benefits at all. So certainly, His plan for marriage to be honored and kept pure is nothing short of perfect.

Chapter 2

SELF LESS

can remember a time when I was having a little pity party about being an at-home mom. The very thing that I had prayed to be able to do I was now complaining about. God is so good for putting up with me. Anyhow, I was in the middle of dealing with something that Blaise, our third child, was going through, and I had become frustrated with him not accepting the help I had offered to him. After some time, I backed off so that he could reap the consequences of his decision. Well, in the end he decided to take my help, and as a result overcame his hurdle.

When this happened, I got a revelation—my purpose is what I am doing right this moment. My husband teaches physics to high school students. I teach life skills to our children. I guess I never thought about the fact that what I do has significant impact. It's like I was equating meaningful work with an income and a building outside of my home. But God made it plain to me right then and there that what I do at home in a pair of sweatpants *is* important and *is* work.

For far too long I believed that the season I am in of raising kids was something that I had to complete before I could move on to doing ministry. Now I realize that raising my kids is ministry. I have a children's ministry! God has granted the privilege of rearing four young people steeped in sin, given to a couple steeped in sin, and saved only by the grace of God through Jesus Christ—not only to raise them, but to train them to follow Him. Talk about mission impossible. But according to Philippians 4:13, all things *are* possible through Him who strengthens me. In earlier chapters of this same book of the Bible we are given additional wisdom.

Do nothing out of selfish ambition or vain conceit. Rather in humility, value others above yourselves, not looking to your own interests but each of you to the interests of others. (Philippians 2:3-4)

These verses about selflessness—or selfishness, depending on how you look at it—are ones that Ross and I had to memorize when we were going through marriage counseling. However, they apply to parenting as much as they do to matrimony.

Have you ever felt like you have so many things to do, but very few of those things are what you want to do? Below is something I journaled one day when I was feeling fed up with giving myself to everyone but myself.

I'm having one of those days. I want to work on the books that I'm writing. I want to call a friend and catch up. I want to read a book that someone gave me yesterday. But right next to my list of "want to's" is a big 'ole list of "have to's" that jumps ahead of the former list, looking back only to wag its tongue. The few precious hours I have during the day when Story is asleep must be rationed and prioritized

*to make the most of them. This being the case, the laundry
goes into the washing machine and my writing is resigned
to this one paragraph that I have just written.*

Being a resident parent (one who has dependent
children living with them) is a selfless season of life. But
I can guarantee that once you leave this season, there
will be a time that you will long for it again. As you see a
couple with a little girl, you think longingly back to your
days of parenting your daughter at that age; or as you
pass a little league field, you feel an aching in your heart
to revisit being in the bleachers, cheering your son on with
the other team families. The reason I know is because I
have heard from people time and time again about how
they miss "those days." They say things like, "It goes by
too fast" or "Enjoy them while they're still young" or "I wish
I had it to do all over again. "

Returning to that Scripture in Philippians, it later reads,

In [Chanty's] *relationship with* [others], *have the same
mindset as Christ Jesus: Who, being in very nature God,
did not consider equality with God something to be used
to his own advantage; rather he made himself nothing by
taking the very nature of a servant, being made in human
likeness. And being found in appearance as a man, he
humbled himself by becoming obedient to death-even
death on a cross!* (Philippians 2:5-8)

I don't know if "Chanty" is in your Bible but it's in mine.
You see, I crossed out "your" and replaced it with my
name. Some time ago a woman who led me and some
other ladies through a Bible study shared about this
practice. For me it is a reminder that what I read isn't just

general requests but specific commands to me, Chanty, to obey. Often I would read Scripture and feel that it applied to other people. But replacing "you" or "your" with "Chanty" reminds me that God is talking directly to me.

So, to have the attitude of Christ as I raise my children means:

1. Not being a replacement for God in their lives

How does this all translate into action, especially when the parent is to be the authority in a child's life? Well, let's begin by discussing who's really the authority. Exodus 20:3 says, "You shall have no other gods before me." There are times when we try and help our child when what we truly are doing is hindering God's hand at work in their life. Keeping a toddler protected from every tumble that she may take is not going to prepare her to avoid the big fall around the corner. She needs to experience the discomfort of the minor tumbles to learn to adjust her gait before a major fall happens.

It is almost innate as a parent to want our kids to succeed and do better in life than what we did. But what does *better* mean? Oftentimes we associate it with increased income or social status. However, God tells us that the treasures of this world are not ones with which we should be concerned (Matthew 6:19-21). Our goal may be to get our kids into the best college in the world when God's desire is for them to save the lost in the world. As parents, it is vital that we trust God for our children with all our hearts and not lean to our own understanding of what we think is right.

2. Making myself nothing, akin to the nature of a servant

Having worked as a nurse, I know a thing or two about servanthood. I can recall one patient who regularly insisted that her constipation be relieved manually. As her nurse, like it or not, this duty (no pun intended) was my responsibility. It was part of my service to my patient. Likewise, as a parent, we are responsible for serving our children. This is no easy task. I remember the days, weeks, and early months after delivering our first child, Morgan. I was EX-HAU-STED. It was like I was her 24-hour attendant. I breastfed her, changed her, held her, bathed her, comforted her, watched her, and studied her. I took her with me everywhere I went. My body was not my own. I shared it with her.

Now that she is older, I don't have as much, if any, physical responsibility for her, but she still requires help to navigate the world around her. Children (young or old) don't instinctively do the hard things in life without some coaching and guidance. For this reason, Ross and I need to be on-call to train them at a moment's notice, which is not always convenient or expected. Countless times we have lamented to one another about how our time is not our own.

As much as I think I know about servanthood, Jesus knows way more. His body was *literally* not His own. He became human, yet He is God. He donned a body of flesh and lived among us. Jesus surrendered His deity, His supernatural being, to be a human. Like a parent, He laid down Himself to nurture and sustain the lives of us, His children. He experienced joy, pain, heartache, and grief all without sinning. It is our privilege to experience just a taste of the sacrifice that our Lord and Savior endured.

3. Humbling myself in obedience

It is embarrassing having to enforce the punishment that I've fashioned for my kids on myself, but it's come to pass on several occasions. And boy, do they love when it happens!

Humility is not comfortable. Humility as a parent is even more uncomfortable. I guess it's because I think that I should not be messing up in front of my kids. I'm supposed to be calm, cool, and collected. So, when I have those moments of flying off the handle or doing something out of sorts (like singing at the dinner table which is a no-no in our home) I get embarrassed and want to save face. After all I'm Mommy the Great.

Despite my natural instinct to grab hold of my pride, the greatest gift I can give to my kids is to throw it to the ground. Only in that position can they see what should be elevated — humility. God says in His Word that He opposes the proud but gives grace to the humble (James 4:6). How can I as a parent know this truth, not put it into practice, and then expect my kids to believe God's Word? Let them see me humbled, embarrassed, wrong, out of sorts, because if I do it right, they're going to also see the grace of God. In this way, they'll know that His grace is for them as well.

A simple way to demonstrate humility is to ask for forgiveness from your child when circumstances warrant doing so. Be bold enough to ask them publicly when necessary. Seeing you do so models God's Word plainly. Even if you do it late, even if you do it secretly because of embarrassment, just do it. Your actions are still teaching them. *Dad sure was uncomfortable telling me he was sorry. I guess if I feel uncomfortable saying sorry, it's okay.*

4. Dying

Thank God, Jesus died so we don't have to die! However, you and I both know there are times when we feel what I term "mini-deaths." Compare, if you will, a stroke to a mini-stroke or TIA (transient ischemic attack). In the case of a stroke, a blood clot is actively preventing blood flow by blocking an artery leading to the brain. With a mini-stroke, the same thing happens, however the blockage is temporary and blood flow returns. Such is the case with us.

Having a newborn, dealing with a wayward child, trudging through a season of single parenting, even having to give the job priority over your child all feel comparable to loss. What an opportunity to show our children how to navigate these temporary struggles or even how it's okay to grieve through them! It's easy for kids to believe they've experienced things because they've seen them on social media. But there's a clear difference between seeing and living. The former yields information; the latter yields wisdom.

I tend to go off by myself when I am disturbed to the point of tears, thinking, *I don't want the kids to worry about me.* The only time they normally see me cry is during church when I'm moved by the Holy Spirit through a song or testimony. Wouldn't it be interesting to think that our kids are worried about us because they *don't* see us cry?

Child to a friend: *"Yeah, I think my mom is an alien. I've never seen her shed a tear."*

What an impact it would make for our children to see us dying to self (putting off our natural instinct to save face) and become vulnerable (allow Holy Spirit to reign no matter what that looks like). I believe that for them to see us going through trials while looking to God is invaluable.

Several years back I had the privilege of being one of the speakers during our church's Good Friday service. Public speaking has never ranked highly on my bucket list. Ever since grade school I have struggled with giving speeches and talking in front of people in general. However, God had been speaking to me about facing this fear and, around this time, His voice was getting really loud. So, when I was asked to speak, I already knew the answer was "Yes."

Mind you that after agreeing, I also found out that I would have to memorize my entire message. AAAAAGH! Added pressure. Now my stomach was in knots. But as usual I kept my feelings to myself. I thought, *Me and Jesus can handle this. I'm not going to tell anyone I'm nervous. I'm just going to be a good Christian and go to Him.*

Well, believe it or not, I had just addressed this very issue in my marriage. I had been keeping my feelings about my husband's shortcomings to myself, causing me to grow bitter towards him. God had already spanked my hand for that and said, "Chanty, enough!" Now I was plotting to use the same errant practice in this situation. *Whaat?!* "No," I said almost out loud. I'm going to tell people that I'm scared and to pray for me.

The people I told included my family and specifically my kids. At our meal times whoever is leading the prayer asks for prayer requests. I said, "Mommy's going to be a speaker at Good Friday service this year. I am scared about speaking in front of people. In the past my voice has been shaky, and I get extremely nervous. Can you please pray that I would speak with power and without fear?" It was hard to say this in front of my kids. It was hard to let them know that I was scared about something. I don't know why, but it was. My family prayed for me that day and beyond that day. When Good Friday came, and God delivered His message through me with power and without fear, they saw His power in my weakness (2 Corinthians 12:9). By way of my mini-death, my children saw life.

Chapter 3

TRANSITIONING

Four years ago, I went through a process with my hair called "transitioning." Ever since I was a young girl, my hair had been chemically straightened (or relaxed) to better manage its kinky texture. In its relaxed state I could run a comb through it with ease, pull it back into a ponytail, as well as go into a body of water and come out looking presentable. Well, there's this growing trend where Black women have been either keeping their hair in its natural kinky state or reverting to their hair's natural kinky state. Since I had lived my life getting my hair relaxed, to engage in this trend I had to do the latter. There were two options for me to go about this process:

1. Cut off all my relaxed hair and start growing my hair from scratch
2. Transition by growing out my natural hair and gradually trimming away my straightened hair

I opted for the latter because I'm a chicken. I couldn't fathom being without my hair that took me all the way until my mid-20s to properly grow. Transitioning provided me with the time I needed to adjust to losing some of my hair length while still achieving the goal of growing out my kinky hair. In other words, I was preparing for the future under the protection of the present.

My hair scenario sums up what I'll be discussing in this chapter. For children to grow into well-adjusted adults, they too need to undergo transition. This process lets them practice independence while they are still dependents. It can be nerve-wracking because we parents are witnesses to their many mistakes while they're still under our roof. But ultimately, it's better than witnessing a mistake outside the home that they were never taught could be avoided.

Baby

Transitioning starts as early as infancy. I shared in Chapter 1 that keeping a baby in your bedroom is a set up for dependency. To clarify, this is regardless of whether you are a married couple or a single parent. The concept of boundaries begins within the context of the family. Then later it can be more easily understood and applied to the world. Think about how easily kids learn the word "mine." Yes, we teach them to share, but it is also okay to teach them that some things are not shared.

Something that can be tough for parents is letting their kids self-soothe. I remember our kids' pediatrician teaching us about the importance of this concept. Infants can learn to satisfy themselves *if we give them the opportunity.* We take away this opportunity if we go into their rooms (that is *if* they are in their own room) and pick them up as soon as we hear a cry. Instead of us training them, they're training us. No, we don't ignore every cry. Crying is a baby's way of telling us he's hungry, needs changed, or is uncomfortable.

But babies also cry when they're bored, missing you, and just because. So, our job is to diagnose and treat. If we don't see any issue of import, then we need to back off and see how she does on her own. I recall reading a parenting book a few years back where the author talked about how he would stand outside his infant daughter's room when she was crying and wait. As soon as there was a pause in the crying, he would immediately go in and scoop her up. This is called positive reinforcement. He was training her by rewarding her for when she stopped crying. Being consistent in this practice can promote self-soothing in babies.

Toddlers

Toddlers are tricky. Sometimes they want mommy and other times they want to rule. The inner struggle of toddlers and preteens can seem like one and the same. The training you provide during infancy will lay the groundwork for the tricky toddler years. Prepare for boundaries to be tested inside and outside of the home. Along with the breakneck speed with which we see them developing physically, they are developing psychologically at an equally dizzying speed. Their minds are discovering what is true. If I touch this stove, what will it feel like? How does the dog react when I jump on him? When I run away from Daddy in the store what will he do? Does flopping on the floor and screaming get me what I want? If I drop this carrot from my highchair a billion times will my sister pick it up a billion times? Inquiring minds want to know! And hopefully you don't lose your mind in the process.

Once again, I bring up the word consistency. I'm going to go out on a limb and venture to say that you enjoy stability. You want to feel secure. You are happiest when your life is steady and comfortable. This same bent that you have as an adult is what a child craves. They best function and thrive under a set rhythm of life. Guess who sets that rhythm. Their parents. We do this by guiding them through daily routines. These routines provide answers to their many questions **AS LONG AS THE ROUTINES ARE CONSISTENT**. If routines are variable, then all bets are off. Surely you've heard of bedtime routines or morning routines. But I want you to see that your responses to your child are also routines.

As an example, when we began training Story to poop in the potty, there was a song and dance I did to celebrate. He expected that song and dance every time. I used it to positively reinforce his good choice of choosing to poop in the potty rather than in his underwear. In the same way, the first time Morgan stepped down off a step, Ross and I let out a resounding cheer. For the next several weeks, she wouldn't step down off a step without first getting our attention, pausing for dramatics, and then stepping down. Can you guess what we did in response? Cheer, of course! So, in both examples, a routine is in place for positive behavior.

There should also be routines set for negative behavior. Toddlers are infamous for throwing tantrums. A routine could be a two-minute time out for a tantrum. Toddlers are also known for looking at a parent before doing something they know they shouldn't do. You know the look. A routine could be a hug, an affirmation, or a treat if they make the choice to practice self-control rather than pull the cat's tail.

Alternatively, routines like rescuing and excusing may negatively impact a child's behavior. Rescuing looks like this. Johnny looks at the cat. Johnny looks at you. Johnny reaches to pull the cat's tail and Daddy scoops Johnny up. Dad may do this for one of two reasons:

1. He does not want Johnny to reap the consequence of getting scratched by the cat

2. He does not want to take the time to discipline Johnny for doing something wrong

In a nutshell, Dad's motives are either to rescue Johnny or himself: Johnny from harm; himself from the work of discipline. Our cat does not have claws, but she does bite. There have been times when we've let our cat bite Story because Story chose to keep bothering her. Yes, he cried, but, more importantly, he learned. The lesson taught itself. This doesn't work for all situations like letting a child near a swimming pool or putting him in some other life-threatening scenario. But, when it's plausible, the best time to let our children fall is under our watch so that they can avoid the bigger pitfalls of life away from our guidance.

"He needs a nap." "She's used to playing with older kids." "He's very emotional." Excuses. You've used them before. I have, too, but they are not my normal routine. If my child makes a bad choice, he is responsible for making things right. This may be an apology, cleaning up, or giving something up. Excusing his behavior teaches him that he's not responsible for his own actions—I am. And I'm certainly not going to claim any of the crazy choices my children make when there are enough crazy choices that I make on my own. Teach your toddler the practice of humbling herself at this early age and she will be on a course that leads to freedom.

Preschool

Preschoolers are in an extremely teachable season of life. Where infants and toddlers are learning much by observation, preschoolers are maturing in communication. It's a time when you can finally understand what they are saying, and they are able to verbalize understanding of what you're saying to them. This is the age when we begin giving our children household responsibilities and an allowance. One does not coincide with the other, but because two-way communication is at a premium during this stage, it is a good time to introduce these practices. You may ask, "What kind of chores can a 3-year-old do?" My response would be:

- *Make their bed*
- *Load and unload the dishwasher*
- *Put dirty clothes in a drawstring bag and pull them to the laundry room to wash*
- *Put clean clothes away in drawers*
- *Bring groceries in from the car*
- *Help wash the vehicle*
- *Set the dinner table*
- *Put extra toilet paper rolls in the bathrooms*

There are many tasks they can do and even enjoy doing. If you begin putting them to work at this age when work seems like a game, when they're older it will be (here's that word again) **routine** for them. Now, I must give you a disclaimer—the above list may not be done to your specifications. The bed won't be made like you would make it. A dish may break. A tire brush may be mistakenly used while cleaning the fender of your SUV. Be mindful that most of these chores are not to be done independently from you but, rather, along with you. The goal is conditioning them with a good work ethic in preparation for the future.

I mentioned providing an allowance during the preschool years. In our home allowance is not a reward or incentive. It is used to teach our kids about how money works. Each week they receive a dollar amount equal to their age. There's also a routine for what they do with their money. First, they give a tithe (10%) to God. Then, they put away half of what remains into a savings account. Finally, they keep the other half of what remains for spending. Doing this allows for teaching on many different levels. Biblically we can share what the Bible says regarding tithing, spending, and saving. Delayed gratification is taught as our kids see something in a store or at a friend's house and begin the process of sacking money away for what they desire. And one of my favorite lessons, frugality, comes into play as they come to understand how expensive things can be and pursue creative avenues for getting something at a price they can afford.

At this age, receiving the same allowance for a whole year makes for great math lessons. They see the same coins and hear the same amounts for an extended period. During this time, you can reinforce what each coin is called.

For Story, at the time of this writing, 40 cents is the tithe because it's 10% of his allowance. When I work with Story to put his tithe in the envelope, I'll say to him, "Okay, Story, pick out the nickel." "Where's the dime?" Whether he picks right or not, over time he's learning to identify the various coins and eventually learning their value individually and collectively. Once again, providing opportunity is the first step.

Early School Years

Independence during the elementary school years comes with the territory. As you wave good-bye to them from the bus stop, you're also waving good-bye to being the sole major influence in their lives. At this stage, peers and school teachers begin to grapple for equal footing with parents. This is only natural since most kids spend more waking hours of the weekdays in school than they do at home. I remember hearing our kids say, "That's not what Mrs. Smith says" or "Patrick's got a Nintendo DS. Can I have one, too?" During these years, more than ever, it was important for us to have routines that kept our children mindful of our family's structure so they weren't pining away for somebody else's. Following are some practices we began to use to promote age-appropriate independence in our children.

As the kids developed friendships in school, they were invited to birthday parties. We developed the rule that if they went to a birthday party, they had to pay for the gift.

My book, *Personal Finances Personal Freedom* (PFPF)[1], shares about how our children tackled this task. Doing this puts the onus on them to pursue what they want to do. They are the ones who want to attend the party, so they are the ones who should put forth the time, forethought, and finances. The critical thinking involved in managing time and money have provided valuable lessons for our kids that spill into other areas of their lives.

Our kids are responsible for waking up on time for school. I can hear some people right now saying, "If I didn't wake my child up, she'd never go to school." Yes, she would. If the consequences from you, her school, and her peers mean anything to her, she would. And if not, maybe they're not the right consequences. (See Chapter 5.)

For ten years I was a homemaker, and although I didn't enjoy taking my kids to school, I was available to do it if need be. But there were times when I've had them call a neighbor, friend, or friend's parent for a ride. I believe there was even a time when one of our kids walked to or from school. And, yes, there have been times when a child, after sleeping in, has made the decision to stay home—multiple times. But eventually, the pressure and the consequences became so great that he opted to make getting to school his goal.

It is hard to take when they miss a day of school because of being late. We got close to the point of having an intervention due to tardiness and missed days. But I

---

1 Chanty Webb, *Personal Finances Personal Freedom,* Olive Press Publisher, 2013.

was proactive. When I saw my child digging his heels in, I reached out to the guidance counselor to inform her of the situation. This way our son was being held accountable both inside and outside of our home. Yes, some grades took a hit because of classwork that was missed. But my focus is not on today's grade, it's on tomorrow's man. This boy needs to be trained in a routine now so that he can grow into a man later.

Continuing on the topic of school, our children have been lunch packers right from the start. This began as early as kindergarten when they helped with this task. I share in PFPF that they were instructed as to what goes into a lunch. So as 5-year olds they learned what a lunch is composed of:

- *A sandwich or other entrée (possibly leftovers)*
- *A salty snack (like chips or pretzels)*
- *A fruit or "sweet" (like yogurt or oatmeal bar)*
- *A water bottle*

Eliminating the guesswork of what's for lunch makes it a breeze for them to do it themselves. We sometimes provide specified quantities of items for their lunches so that they don't go overboard on calories and so they don't plow through our groceries in one week. Setting these quantities adds to the ease of preparation.

One final topic I want to address as kids transition into this stage is handling offenses. If one of our children disrespected someone (babysitter, friend, teacher, bus driver), they would make it right by writing a letter of apology. There was even an occasion that one of our kids had to read their letter aloud in front of peers. In this day and age, writing letters is considered old school, so part of the consequence was the tedious nature of the task—having to manually write something out. But it always amazes me how genuine the kids' expressions of repentance are on paper. I think there's something to be said for the reflection and mental muscle that goes into the task of writing. Thoughts being transferred from heart to head to hand involves a process that goes deeper than what we even realize. Our kids may not understand that process, but the fruit it yields is priceless.

Middle School

See "Toddler Years."

Just kidding. Seriously though, it's as if tweens are in this weird holding place sandwiched between childhood and adulthood. They want to act like kids, yet they want to be treated like adults.

Give me a hug, Mom. ... But not in public.

Talk to me, Dad. ... But not when my friends are around.

I want pizza. ... I'm only eating salad.

Yay, you rented a Power Rangers DVD! ... Power Rangers is for little kids.

Can I have a Dora bandage on my boo-boo? ... I don't need anything on my cut.

Arggh! Which end is up?

I'll never forget what my husband once told me: Even when they act like they don't want to be touched or held, do it anyway. Ross is a high school teacher. He sees kids on a daily basis who play tough but actually are suffering inside because they aren't getting the affection they so desperately need. So, I listened. The hardest child for me to follow through on with this was Morgan—our only girl. Especially in middle school, I just felt like she wanted no part of me. I expected her to instinctively recoil anytime I would go to embrace her. When some daughters' moms came around, I would see them run to their mom and give them a hug even in front of their friends. When I came around, Morgan would acknowledge me respectfully or just quickly wave hello. You can imagine how it was difficult for me to actively seek out affection when I felt as though it was not invited. I did my best, but I don't feel that I was successful in being affectionate with her. Quite honestly, I was so wrapped up in feeling inadequate about her response to me, that I couldn't practice the important task of showing her physical love. Don't make that same mistake. Listen to Ross—do it anyway.

I found affection easier with the boys. Blaise often comes to me, puts his arm around me and asks, "Can I have a hug?" It doesn't get any easier than that. Hunter is a little more complicated. Because he's not a touchy-feely kind of guy, I will actively pursue him. I used to make a point of going to him before I retired for the night to give him a hug. Other times I'd playfully tug at him or wrap my arms around him. I liken it to sneaking vegetables in a child's food. You give them something they need but don't want without them knowing you're giving it to them. And every once in a while, (probably about three times a year to be exact) he'd say to me, "Can I have a hug?" That's the go ahead for me to lay on him all that's been held back for the other 362 days of the year.

These are the years when children begin to feel more of the weight of their choices. Therefore, it is more important than ever to **let that weight rest on them**. Here's a good example of this:

Morgan had started performing in the high school marching band during her last year of middle school. Summer band camp had two-a-day practices and one day we went swimming at a friend's house in between. When it was time to leave from our friend's home, Morgan said to me, "Mom, can I go home and take a shower?" It was a half hour before the start of practice. This meant she could not go home, take a shower, and make practice on time. I responded by saying, "Yes, you can go home and take a shower, but you will probably be late for band camp." She thought about it for a couple seconds and said, "Never mind. I'll just go to practice." That was a good mom moment. It doesn't always go that way. But this time it was easy because the choice was hers and the consequences were hers. Morgan's peers in the saxophone section and her band directors would put the pressure on her if she showed up late. She knew this without even going down that road. So, she reasoned on her own that showing up on time (albeit a little smelly) was better than showing up late and smelling like a rose.

It doesn't always go that smoothly though. And when it doesn't, when those natural consequences make you wince for your child, be their good Samaritan. They've already received their discipline, so this is your opportunity to love them up and comfort them. Tell them you still love them and that God still loves them, too. Show them scripture to prove those truths. (Hebrews 12:5-11 is a great one.) Then let them know they can move on because God does not condemn them (Romans 8:1-2).

As they are maturing with accepting responsibility for themselves, they can also take on more responsibility for the family. Our children began cooking in some form or fashion around 8-10 years of age. As a tween, children can move beyond helping with meal prep to fully preparing meals. Who can't follow the instructions on a box of Hamburger Helper? If you've been training them by having them watch you in the kitchen as you brown meat and use the appliances, they should be poised to have an assigned day of the week to cook during this stage of their life.

Another responsibility we've put on our children is communicating via an email account. The primary purpose was to ask questions of and give responses to their teachers. But sometimes they would receive correspondence through extracurricular activity groups and from us as their parents regarding issues concerning them. For example, if we see something at the library or if someone asks a question about them through us, we give them the opportunity to follow up instead of us doing it for them. Most of our kids started an email account before middle school, but since some providers won't allow anyone younger than 12 to create an account, I included the topic under middle school years.

On a side note, I can remember an occasion when our neighbor came over to the house. He was picking up the mail we had collected for him for the two weeks that he and his wife had been out of town. When he came into the house, Blaise was sitting at the kitchen table doing homework. From where our neighbor Miguel stood in the hallway, he could see Blaise at the table and said, "Hello" to him. Blaise said "Hello" back and then he did something unexpected. He got up from the table, walked over to where Miguel was standing, and put his hand out to shake Miguel's hand. It was evident through his body language and his expression to Blaise that Miguel was impressed by this act. Typically, when Miguel greets my son, he responds sheepishly, barely making eye contact with him and talking to him in a very quiet voice. But with this encounter Miguel saw a change in Blaise. With this simple response, Blaise displayed that he was transitioning from a boy into a man.

High School

Ah, the high school years. At this stage I remember finally feeling relaxed enough to let the chips fall where they may—most of the time. But after several years of transitions it was much easier to fully let them shoulder the load than it would have been had we waited until this point to do so. Little by little they had been given responsibility. Little by little we had let go of responsibilities. In doing so, independence increased and dependence decreased. The result was growing confident children capable of moving into adulthood.

At this point in the game we basically passed the baton of life over to them. Here's what that looks like.

The choice to study, do homework, and make up classwork falls on them. Gone are the days of checking behind them to see that assignments are completed. Or making them study days leading up to a test. It's their choice. That choice comes with consequences of either success or failure. Being eligible or ineligible. Going to the college of their choice or the only college that will accept them. We still check grades. We still have discussions about school, but we don't mandate action. That's the difference. Following are some example circumstances in which we force our teens to act independently of us.

Our children began filling out health forms in middle school so that they would know as much about their health history as I did. As they moved into high school, I began to have them see the doctor without me in the room. I knew that, because of their age, certain topics would be addressed like sexual activity or specific vaccinations. With this in mind, I would have conversations with them ahead of the appointment to discuss these crucial topics together.

Following this preparation, my absence forced them to use their words. That's an expression that you hear moms saying to little kids all the time. "Tyler, use your words." In other words, whatever alternative expression Tyler is using is not cutting it. Tyler needs to talk for his own good so that he learns to communicate in an acceptable way with others. Taking mom or dad out of the equation in the doctor's office puts the responsibility on the teen to effectively communicate the status of her health. They will soon be doing this on their own should they leave the home after graduation. It's good practice to put them in the position of taking on this responsibility prior to that time.

Coming of age also provided the opportunity for our kids to be more financially independent. There was a point in time when our two older kids started buying the clothes they needed or wanted. We didn't even ask them to; they just did it. Then our oldest son, Hunter, ever the spendthrift, came to us one day to let us know that he needed socks. We'd gotten used to them buying their own clothing and he always has a big wad of money in his wallet, so Ross asked him, "Why can't you buy them? You buy all your other stuff." Hunter lightly protested, "Yeah I buy the stuff I want but you guys are responsible for the basics like underwear and socks." That's Hunter. Our play-by-the-rules child. The benefit runs both ways in that we had a little less out of our pocket and our kids more fully appreciated the value of stuff.

Once they began to drive, they paid the increase in our insurance cost. Additionally, they provided gas money when they use the car for work or pleasure. They also purchase their own cell phones and pay for their cell phone bills. These practices meld together to prepare them for the bills and expenses they will soon have as they venture out into life on their own.

The reason they had some degree of financial independence is the direct result of working a job. Both our teens pursued jobs even before they got their work permits. Working has truly helped them grow up as a result of having to be accountable to someone outside the home. There is no sheltering a teen from the consequences of workplace irresponsibility. This is a *good* thing. What a wonderful training field for their future lives as adults! Running late? You have to communicate that to your boss. Sick? You must call in and submit proof from a doctor that you were sick. Skipped your day to work? You may be fired. This taste of the real world serves a teen well as he navigates the boundaries of interacting with others.

On the topic of the "real world," around ninth and tenth grade our two oldest kids began researching higher education options. Their schools offered college trips to local universities. Outside of this we would also incorporate college visits into our family vacations. Doing so provided the opportunity to check out schools that would normally be out of the way. Even though the kids were as young as 14 and 15 when we did this, the colleges still go out of their way to make a lasting impression. One school even gave vouchers to waive the application fee should they choose to apply. Morgan attended one of the very schools the kids picked to visit in Greenville, South Carolina.

Hunter, however, was determined that he had no need for a college education in the field he was pursuing. We didn't agree with him, but we didn't twist his arm either. Our job was not to push him to do what we wanted him to do. Our job was to give him all the information we knew about his potential decision and its consequences. After doing all we knew to do, we continued to pray and wait on God's final say.

For me, this is one of the toughest parts of parenting— letting my kid's choices play out. Especially when I feel that they're not the best choices. But we must let them be the benefactors or victims of their choices in order for them to learn. Playing interference will only stunt their growth, prevent development, and leave them ill-prepared for real world life. Stay tuned until the end of the book to hear about the outcome of Hunter's decision.

Chapter 4
PASS THE SALT

If there's one thing I cannot stand, it is bland food. There's nothing worse than biting into a piece of baked chicken that looks good and well-seasoned on the outside, only to discover it has zero flavor on the inside. I'll eat it out of hunger, but I will not be having seconds and I am not getting any pleasure from consuming it. On the other hand, food that's been well-seasoned piques my senses. I want to eat every last bit of it, in addition to knowing how the cook prepared it, so that I can make some on my own. Not only will seconds and thirds grace my plate, but I will also tell others about the enjoyment I had in savoring it.

You are the salt of the earth. But if the salt loses its saltiness, how can it be made salty again? It is no longer good for anything, except to be thrown out and trampled underfoot. (Matthew 5:13)

Do you know how we as believers lose our legacy of saltiness? By not passing it along to our children. Complacency is easy. Toeing the line takes work. Daily, hourly, we are responsible for seasoning our kids to taste different to the world. Sometimes I am tempted to turn my back, pretend I didn't see this or that because it means time and effort on my part. *Why can't they just run on auto-pilot?* I've thought to myself. The fact is kids don't. So, I need to hunker down, get in that co-pilot seat, and buckle up for the ride.

Prayer

In the course of raising preschoolers into children, there are many things we were intentional about and many things that we just did on the fly. One of the more intentional practices was teaching our kids to pray. First, we modeled it. Before every meal and before bed at night, we would pray with our kids. Other times, as a need would arise for a family member or friend, our kids would hear us pray on the phone for the person or see us lay hands on them and pray right then and there. They would then mimic. First bowing their head and folding their hands. Then listening. And finally, patiently waiting until the prayer was over so that they could emphatically agree, "Amen!" I fondly remember our daughter Morgan being seated at the head of the dining room table in my in-loves' home. Several relatives were gathered around to celebrate her first birthday. Following my reading aloud of each birthday card, she would exclaim, "Amen!" Boy did our relatives love that and boy did Morgan know it! But more importantly, she had learned about prayer and that it could be done at anytime and anywhere.

For the Bible Tells Me So

We believe that Biblical teaching needs to begin in our home. The church is not responsible. The schools are not responsible. God plainly puts the responsibility on parents in His Word.

These commandments that I give you today are to be on your hearts. Impress them on your children. Talk about them when you sit at home and when you walk along the road, when you lie down and when you get up. Tie them as symbols on your hands and bind them on your foreheads. Write them on the doorframes of your houses and on your gates. (Deuteronomy 6:6-9)

When our children were young (and now for Story) we used music, children's Bibles, Veggie Tale DVDs, and even Biblical radio dramas to reach them with the Gospel message. I think the radio dramas were one of their favorite ways of hearing God's Word. God's timing is perfect in that they aired during the time we were driving to Bible study at our church. The stories are about kids around their age who inevitably encounter some sort of conflict where they need to make a tough choice.

At the end of the broadcast, the show's host recounts the story and shares scripture pertaining to the episode. There have been times when the kids didn't want to go into church because they were so wrapped up in a story. As a mom, it feels good to "sneak" the Good News into them in this manner, kind of like how I used to have to sneak zucchini into meals at dinnertime. They enjoy the program *and* are getting the Word of God planted into their hearts.

I would love to tell you that we read the Bible with our children every day since they were born, but that would be a lie. I tried reading the Bible to Morgan and Hunter when they were preschoolers. It wore me out. I guess I was expecting them to be engaged; and they were at times. But most times they were doing what kids do—anything other than listening to me. I gave up. But what I have done is to make sure they see me reading my Bible. My prayer is that they recognize that if Mom's reading on a regular basis it must be important to do so. In the past we have had the kids commit to memorizing Scripture or reading their Bibles for a certain amount of time. We may revisit this in the future. For right now, I believe it is important for them to see us reading the Word of God and that this will lead them to read it.

Church Fellowship

I cannot say enough about how impactful our church has been for us as a family. It is family to us. God has birthed us into families whom we love and who love us. He has also given us an extended family of believers in Him who are committed to living out His Word daily. We have relationship with these people based on the choice we made individually to receive Jesus into our lives.

For us the church is not limited to the building on the property where we worship on Sundays and attend Bible study on Wednesdays. The church also includes the people we encounter there and elsewhere whose hearts are aligned with God's. Those souls who serve, worship, and delight in the Savior Jesus Christ are the church—and they continue to touch our lives daily.

Wise Counsel

I don't believe that Ross and I would be married today if it weren't for our church. During our 22 years as a wedded couple, we have encountered struggles with pornography, financial brokenness, a defiant child, opposite work schedules, unexpected pregnancies, lack of sexual fulfillment, underemployment, and a slew of additional marital issues that could fall under the divorce category of "irreconcilable differences." Having God's Word and fellow believers, who had encountered these same struggles, helped us to take our eyes off ourselves and fix them on God. Our children, although unaware of most of these struggles, still have a sense of the need for the church body. They have heard our conversations with Christians about spiritual things. They have seen people in our lives who have been transformed by Jesus. They have learned scriptures that stress the importance of a relationship with Jesus to navigate life. Through these varied exposures, the kids have experienced firsthand why we invite other believers in to do life alongside of us.

Extended Family

Early on we realized that being a part of the church we were attending (and now have been members of for over 20 years) means more than just seeing members twice a week. Instead our relationships extend beyond the four walls. I'll never forget how Ross and I felt like we were being stalked because it seemed like wherever we went someone from DaySpring (our church) was always around. We'd be in the parking lot about to head into a department store when, "Hello guys!" a friendly voice would croon from across the lot. We would be sitting in a restaurant having dinner and the next thing you know, "Ross and Chanty!" Two tables over another couple is smiling, excited to see us. Eventually I got used to it and realized that the church members had always been around, but never had relationship with me until now. Now that we were a part of the church body, there was recognition and the recognition gave way to permission to enter our lives.

What has this looked like? It is the counsel that we have received from trusted friends and will continue to receive in years to come. It is also reciprocal in that others call on us in times of need. In our children's lives, it has meant having additional paternal figures available when we cannot be around. Ross and I have made a point of the two of us getting away at least twice a year. On multiple occasions, someone from our church family has stayed with our kids to tend to their needs. Words cannot express how valuable this service is to us, not to mention how vital it is to our marriage relationship. As I shared in the first chapter, we cannot be good parents if our relationship as husband and wife is in shambles. "Us" needs to be before "them." Having these helpers come to our house and watch our children provides us with the peace of mind to get away without worry. We know that they are in good hands, they know our children, and they are caring for them because they love them.

Beyond caring for our children in our absence, this extended family also ministers to our children in our presence. It is common for members to share encouraging words directly to our children or to us about our children that we later share with them. As a parent, it is entirely too easy to focus on my children's shortcomings. So, when I hear someone praising them, it reminds me to change my focus from the nitpicky to the bigger picture. In doing so, I realize that I truly am blessed to have my children.

Confidence Building

Attending a physical church has brought about invaluable life experiences. Our children have given personal testimonies, performed, and spoken on the spot before the congregation. These types of public opportunities are often uncomfortable for a child. What a blessing it has been to watch their church family lavish them with love during these times! It allows them to become comfortable and gain confidence before an audience in a safe, encouraging environment.

Service

Being part of church ministry has been instrumental in teaching our kids responsibility. As they serve in different ministries, such as dance, custodial services, and choir, they are subject to an adult who is not their parent. Their responsibility is to do the work of the ministry in a manner that would warrant a paycheck, actually in an even more meticulous manner (Colossians 3:23-24). Talk about life lessons! Humility, selflessness, timeliness, patience, self-control, diligence, accountability—just to name a few. These character traits are not only desirable in future work life, they are essential as a child of God.

One Sunday service during our greeting time, a member of our church's congregation waved me over to where he was seated. I came over and greeted him with a hug. He proceeded to tell me that he had been observing our son, Hunter. "I see his dedication to serving even as a young man. I asked the Lord 'What should I do to bless him?' and the Lord told me to give him $100." Right then and there the man handed me a check for Hunter. Certainly, Ross and I have affirmed the kids in the capacities in which they serve. But when someone else sees their good works and responds in such a profound way, it tends to speak even more clearly. This type of life lesson can only be orchestrated by God.

Worship

It seems that in society these days, we worship ourselves more than we do anyone or anything else. So much of social media is centered around lifting ourselves up. Attending church with our kids has taught them what it looks like to lift Jesus up. Not only is this seen in the music, but it is seen in people giving of their time, talent, resources, and lives for the One who is above them. Worship looks like an attorney teaching in youth ministry. It can be a young teen being led by the Holy Spirit in song before a congregation that includes his peers. Worship is a woman dancing with rheumatoid arthritis because God is just so good. It is a strong man brought to tears over his pastor's fatherly love for him. Witnessing true worship develops true worshipers.

Tithing

Personal Finances Personal Freedom shares much of what we have taught our children about tithing. Before they knew how to do it, we did it for them. As babies whenever they received cash, at least 10% would go to the church as a tithe. When they were old enough to learn about tithing, we sat with them as they received allowances and showed them how much went into the tithing envelope. They would write their name on the envelope. Of course as they got older, they prepared their tithe without any help. Furthermore, they did it instinctively. It became natural to them because they have always done it.

It is not uncommon in the church to see a parent give a dollar or two to a child to put into the offering. This certainly is not wrong. Giving an offering is a great thing to do. However, it leads me to wonder if the money the child is giving is a substitute for their tithe. A tithe takes some time to figure out and it may be a sacrifice to give. But when you start a child tithing early on, they don't miss the money because they've been taught that it's not theirs to keep.

When our children receive money, they automatically think about its value after the tithe. It's like when we as adults receive our paychecks. We don't consider our gross pay as our take-home income. After years of earning a paycheck we recognize that many deductions are made and that after those deductions we receive a lesser amount of money. This "net pay" minus the ten percent for tithe is what we then use to plan our spending. As children go through the process of tithing their money *and* see their parents doing the same, it simply becomes the norm.

Youth Programs

In the same way that children gain a sense of belonging from being part of a team, they also gain a sense of belonging being part of a church. Youth programs are an essential piece in making our children feel at home in any church. When we visited other churches, they used to ask, "Do they have a children's church?" I believe kids feel valued when they see that special accommodations have been made just for them.

What I love about our Children and Student Ministry is the passion with which the teachers pursue the kids, not only inside the church but outside of the church. It is not enough to see the kids on Wednesdays and Sundays. Youth teachers will also attend school plays, recitals, sporting events, as well as take the children on special outings. All of this is done in the name of building relationships, which is where real ministry begins.

At our church, I am a member of a ministry that helps people who come to the altar understand why they have come forward. Whether they were moved to come up for prayer, to ask Jesus into their life, or to join the church, our ministry has the privilege of joining in the work that God is doing in an individual's life. Even though we discuss some sensitive issues with them following their decision, it doesn't end there. We have been trained to remain in relationship with the people we've counseled to help them stay the course. This same dynamic is practiced among those adults who serve with our youth. They pursue our children away from the church and meet them where they live.

I appreciate that our children and most of the children I see at our church want to be there. Rarely do I see heads hanging or arms being pulled as they enter the doors. Some younger ones may be hesitant to leave Mommy, or a visiting child may be timid at being around new faces, but those who come regularly are typically excited about being there. In my eyes, this speaks volumes as to what they are receiving from the church body.

The Gospel Message

As wonderful as it is to have Godly people minister to our children, it is no substitute for our responsibility as parents to share with them about Jesus Christ. What a tragedy it would be for me to go through an entire lifetime with my daughter and never once share with her the Gospel of Jesus Christ.

"She goes with me to church. Surely she's heard it already."

Do you always listen to what people say? I don't. I can tune someone out in a heartbeat. We cannot assume that our kids know that they can have a relationship with Jesus or what that even means. Even though we have shared with our kids about Jesus, I will sometimes do "spot checks" because I know how I was when I first came to know the Lord. I often felt that I wasn't saved anymore because of wrongs that I had done. For this reason, it is important to have a recurring conversation with them about this matter of life and death. It's like the sex talk, but even more important. You don't just leave it at one conversation. As matters come up and as questions arise, you revisit the Word of God for truth.

There are several resources that you can find on-line and in print to help you with this conversation. One of my favorite resources is "The Four Spiritual Laws." It is a simple, short booklet that takes about 7 minutes to read through. I would recommend it for children 12 and older. For younger children, Child Evangelism Fellowship is an excellent resource for child-friendly Gospel materials. Children who are non-verbal can still be taught about Jesus. When Story was two-years old, I would simply tell him, "Story, Jesus loves you!" At the time, he had recently learned to say the phrase, "I love you." He knew that it was reserved for special people, like family and close friends who love him. It was not to be used with everyone he meets. In teaching him these distinctions, we began the continuing lesson of how special Jesus is to us.

Chapter 5

"STOP IT RIGHT NOW BEFORE YOU GET YOUR BEATS BUTT!"

I said that. Sleep-deprived by a chaotic schedule and exasperated by argumentative children, I was pushed to my limit. Unfortunately, my intended threat was met with stifled giggles as the kids tried to keep their composure following my verbal faux pas.

Even as new parents, we knew that we needed to discipline our children. Not only is it important for their safety, but it is important for them in understanding authority. If we don't teach them about authority, how can we teach them about God?

When I was a new wife, I read a book by Bunny Wilson called *Liberated Through Submission*.[1] The book is aimed at helping wives to understand what submission looks like and what it doesn't look like. A wife may hear the Bible verses that tell her to submit to her husband and suddenly, she's up in arms. "What do you mean *submit*?" "He's not gonna treat me like a doormat!" "We are equal partners in this marriage!" "Why doesn't he have to submit to me?" In

---

1 P.B. Wilson, *Liberated Through Submission: God's Design for Freedom in All Relationships!* Harvest House Publishers, 2007.

the book, Wilson speaks of how each one of us submits to someone or something every single day. We submit to our boss's requests. We submit to bill collectors. We even submit to stoplights. Why do we submit? We submit to receive benefits and we submit to receive protection. In this same way God, in His perfect (remember the end of Chapter 1) plan for marriage, has declared that it is best for wives to submit to their husbands. (Read Colossians 3:18 to see how God gives allowance to wives whose husbands are not for Him.) As we submit, we receive the benefits and protection that the Bible promises us.

Benefits abound for children who heed their parents' authority—long life, things going well, and a happy mom, to name a few. In addition to these Biblical promises, there is the training that results for life as an adult outside of the home. Home should not only be a playground for children, but a training ground for future adults.

I don't always feel like training. Do you? Life would be so much easier if kids just came programmed to follow the rules. That line, "This hurts me more than it hurts you" is so true. Not necessarily because my heart hurts to spank my kid, but because everything else hurts from a long day and I just want to go to bed. The drama hurts. Putting down what I'm doing to address my kid's issues hurts. Correcting the same wrong behaviors over and over hurts. Bottom line—my kids are selfish...and so am I.

The Bible overflows with verses about discipline. My favorite is Hebrews 12:11, *"No discipline seems pleasant at the time, but painful. Later on, however, it produces a harvest of righteousness and peace for those who have* been trained by it." I love God's frankness. Essentially, He says, "*This is going to hurt. But next time when you're thinking about doing the same dumb thing, you'll remember how your butt feels right now and you won't do it.*"

In other portions of that same passage, He speaks of how **we know we belong to a father when we are disciplined, and we respect him for disciplining us**. In other words:

Discipline=Relationship=Love

Remove the discipline of a child and the relationship with that child is jeopardized, causing the child to feel insecure about being loved. It goes back to the benefits and protection that I spoke of earlier. Suffice it to say that God has it arranged so that we thrive with discipline. Often people believe the contrary: that discipline develops fear and drives wedges in relationships. Abuse yes. Discipline no. We don't have to understand it. We can simply trust in the authority of God's Word and know that it works.

Throughout a child's life, discipline should look different. Take for example our son Story. At 18 months old, he knew he was cute. He knew it because people told him all day long how cute he was. They smiled at him. We would smile at him. We laughed at the things he did. He would wave to people he didn't know, and they would wave right back at him. He was learning all about the power and influence that he had in the world around him.

Cute behaviors aren't the only way he learned. Sometimes he learned by throwing his sippy cup on the floor or hitting me in the face or pulling our cat's tail. These negative behaviors were still a part of his learning, but they required an unpleasant consequence because they are not appropriate behaviors. I hope you get this. When a child, when *your* child misbehaves, they are learning. Think about it like getting a bad grade on a test. Bad grades are a result of:

1. Not knowing all the information
2. Knowing the information and choosing not to apply it

As parents (teachers), we have the responsibility to provide our kids with the information they need to know to get along in the world. This training is called discipline.

DISCIPLINE FOR TODDLERS

Beginning at about 18 months of age, our children's discipline consisted of the following which I will explain in greater detail to follow:

- *Natural consequences*
- *Distraction*
- *Removing attention*
- *Spanking*

Natural Consequences

One morning I was finishing up reading a book that Story had brought to me. He had wandered off into the kitchen and the next thing that I knew I heard a loud THUD followed by even louder crying. I bolted out of my seat, ran around the corner into the kitchen, and found him sprawled out on the floor on his hands and knees. Because I know him so well, I presumed that he had pushed a chair over to the table to try and crawl up on the table and reach something. However, he underestimated the gap between the table and the chair and fell in between the two. I've rescued him from this danger dozens of times, but this time God didn't allow me to do so. Story suffered the consequence of this behavior—pain. No other discipline was needed because he was already suffering. Can you hear the commercial?

"This lesson, 'Crawling Up onto the Table Can Be Painful,' was brought to you by the makers of, 'GRAVITY'!"

Natural consequences are great teachers. Parents need not lift a finger. You get to sit back with your arms crossed and just wait for it. Especially when you are at your wits end...you'll have to forgive me. I feel another commercial coming on.

"At your wits end with disciplining your children? Does the constant questioning of your authority have you worn out? When you're at your wits end, you need 'NATURAL CONSEQUENCES!'" *

* *Only to be used in circumstances where applicable. 'NATURAL CONSEQUENCES is unique to specific situations and is not intended to be the only form of discipline in a child's life. Side effects may include pain, embarrassment, and termination of improper behavior.*

Okay, I'm back. After Story fell from the table, the only thing I needed to do was to comfort him. After a natural consequence is not the time for "rubbing it in." Surely you can have discussion about the choice and the consequence. But no additional punishment should be required. You get to be the good guy by giving love and reassurance.

Distraction

Distraction may not be considered discipline, but it is a part of how we train our kids. The main use of distraction in our household is in teaching patience. I think about a trip our family took to Friendly's once upon a time. Whenever we go out to eat, I look forward to it because it gives me a break from having to plan and prepare a meal. However, with a little guy in tow, the trade-off for that break is crafting a plan to keep him occupied throughout our meal in a public restaurant. There was a television, but at that time our son was not really into television.

So, while we waited for our food, we took him over to the arcade area and let him pretend to play games. During the time when he was at the table, we gave him crayons that the restaurant provides to try and get him to color. We played little games with him that he likes to play at home. I was thankful to God that different friends came by the table to talk because he loves to engage with people outside his family. When all of these measures fail, sometimes we just let him cry because, hey, we're only human.

In my opinion, singing is the ultimate distractor. Each of my kids had "their song" handpicked by Mom that I would use during specific routines or even just for fun. When Hunter was a toddler, "Sesame Street" was a show that he regularly enjoyed. The "Rubber Ducky" song sung by Ernie became his song. I swapped out the lyric:
"Rubber Ducky, you're the one"
for: "Rubber Hunter, you're the one."

The song suited him perfectly because I had a *"little fellow who's cute and yellow and chubby."* (At that part I would tickle his tummy.) Sometimes I would sing it during his bath and other times I would sing it to him on the fly. But it was great for helping him through something that might be somewhat trying for a little one.

Speaking of trying times, let's talk potty training. Distraction through song can be extremely helpful for little ones who aren't interested in sitting still like we are. As adults we may enjoy time on the can because 1) we are taking care of business and 2) it is a nice escape for five minutes or so. But for a toddler who enjoys being on the go to suddenly be placed into a position of being immobile with her bare bottom sitting on a cold hard object, potty-time likely lacks the same appeal. So, we would keep it to five minutes max and try to make it fun with a variety of songs all sung to the tune of a military cadence. Below are some examples.

I go potty everyday
I go potty everyday
'Cause my mom I will obey
'Cause my mom I will obey

It's a party up in here
It's a party up in here
When I go I'll hear a cheer
When I go I'll hear a cheer

(My oldest son was laughing outside the bathroom when I started the refrain for this next verse. You can imagine what he was thinking the ending rhyming word would be.)

On the potty I will sit
On the potty I will sit

It is for my benefit
It is for my benefit

The great part is that you just think up these songs on the fly. You don't have to be any kind of wordsmith. Your kids are going to love whatever songs you sing because they are coming from you as a gift to them. And you are going to love the help it provides you as a parent with getting your child to do what you need them to do.

Here's another one I made up to encourage pa-tience in Story. The song also introduces the concept of patience being a fruit of the Spirit. It goes like this:

Patience is a fruit
Patience is a fruit
When you don't know what to do
Don't know what to do
Patience is a fruit
When you don't know what to do
You sit on the fruit and
WAIT FOR IT!

I sang it to him while his food was being prepared, while his diaper was being changed, and in any other situation where he would get antsy. Our older children picked up on it and would sing it to him when the situation called for it. Ross has even sung it to himself on occasion as a reminder to practice self-control.

Removing Attention

I shared with you earlier how Story knows that he is cute. He gets lots of attention from us and others for being cute. Therefore, we've trained him to expect attention. Taking away this attention is a form of discipline.

When we began having major discipline struggles with our middle son, Blaise, we enrolled in a research study in a local hospital. The investigator was a behavioral psychologist and gave us a ton of helpful information. One of our big take-aways was that we were giving LOTS of attention to our son's negative behavior, but very little attention to his positive behavior. We were instructed to ignore as much negative behavior as possible and make a REALLY big deal over the positive behavior. As we were taught would happen, over time, some of the negative behavior began to extinguish in favor of the positive behavior. We began using this same technique with Story. We gave him the power of influence, but only for positive behaviors. It's not always easy. Has your kid ever done something inappropriate, but it's so funny that you want to bust up laughing? We've had plenty of those moments— with all our kids. But we must practice restraint (most times) so that they can learn that there are rewards for right behavior.

Spanking

We spank our kids.
We spanked our kids.
We have been spanking our kids.
We will be spanking our kids.
We are going to be spanking our kids.
We are spanking our kids.

There. I believe I covered every tense of the word.

Spanking has a time and a place. We believe that the time is when specific behaviors are exhibited. We believe that the place is on the back of the hand when children are younger and, on the buttocks, as they get older. However, if the child chooses to flail around uncontrollably all bets are off.

Humor aside, I realize that the mention of spanking as a form of discipline tends to manifest very strong emotions. There are people who feel that the harm caused to a child by spanking outweigh any disciplinary benefits. Conversely, there are those people who feel that spanking is an invaluable tool in a parent's arsenal of discipline strategies. Ross and I are part of the latter camp. We have made the decision to incorporate spanking along with other forms of discipline previously mentioned to train our children up in the way they should go.

I believe that parents can and do go overboard with spanking. When I say go overboard, I am referring to spanking a child out of anger and without self-control. I am also referring to spanking a child as the primary form of discipline. I have gone overboard in both of those areas. Just like you, I have been learning as I go along, and God has given me the wisdom to see my mistakes and change my behavior.

Around the time our kids turned age one was when they began to get disciplined corporally. In our case, we set the age based on our children's level of understanding. Once it became evident that they understood simple commands, we could safely assume that they were ready to be shaped by this manner of discipline.

We have what we call a "spanking spoon," a little wooden ruler-type instrument, that has been used to give a rap on the hands for misbehavior. The spanking is used after redirection, distraction, and other means of discipline are exhausted. One of my concerns early on as a parent because I am the more sensitive one has been, "What if my child doesn't understand me and I'm spanking her for something she doesn't understand?" That fear was put to rest by the historical accounts of raising four children. I submit to you the following example from several years back.

Ross is in the living room with Story. It's time for bed and books are strewn across the floor. Ross tells him, "Clean up." Story toddles over to a toy, examines it, holds it out to his dad saying something incomprehensible to us. Again, Ross says, "Story, clean up." Story begins jumping, his latest mastered feat which we typically respond to with applause. But this time, the applause ain't comin'.

Ross walks over to him, gives him a swat on his diapered bottom to let him know that he means business and repeats in a daddy voice, "Clean up." (Notice there was no exclamation point. Dads don't need to yell, they just speak, and kids MOVE. I love that about daddies). Story got the message. His books were cleaned up in a heartbeat. Ross praised him and gave him a big hug. After seeing this scenario play out in various instances with our kids, I began to realize that their comprehension was crystal clear.

In the case above, Ross opted to spank Story on the bottom. This is rare as he typically responds to Ross's daddy voice. But when he doesn't, Ross reminds Story that Daddy is in charge.

Story, like many toddlers, went through a phase when he would hurl his cup across the dining room table or backhand his bowl off the table onto the floor. We began spanking him on the hand immediately following the behavior, taking him down from his highchair, and having him clean up. As you can imagine, it was an exhausting, disruptive process to go through night after night. Ross and I began to realize that his behavior was about seeking attention and decided that we would extinguish his behavior based on what we had learned. Instead of making a big deal when he knocked things over, we would completely ignore him, address what needed to be addressed (clean-up that could not wait), and then make him clean up after dinner. If a sippy cup of milk was thrown on the floor, Story would have to wait until after dinner to have any more milk. Natural consequences, baby!

As previously mentioned with the research we participated in, decreased attention equals decreased behavior. After we began ignoring him, Story tapered off the throwing until he finally stopped. *Don't be surprised, however, if new equally disruptive behaviors replace the old ones.* Again, the job of a child is to learn how they affect the world around them and part of their job description includes testing out the limits of the world.

DISCIPLINE
FOR PRESCHOOL AND
YOUNGER SCHOOL AGE CHILDREN

Time Outs

During the research study I mentioned earlier, Ross and I were trained in the discipline technique of time outs. We learned that a time out in the psychology world is the equivalent of a spanking in the Webb world. They taught us to utilize loss of specific privileges for smaller offenses, but a time out was the "big kahuna" of punishments (for ages 2-8). It made me laugh to myself. *A time out is supposed to change our son's behavior? Ha! We'll see about that.*

But amazingly enough, there were times when our son, Blaise, asked for more severe punishments, even a spanking, instead of a time out. Why? First because he is a social kid and interaction with others is what he lives for and second because we made time with us valuable beforehand by being intentional about engaging with him in fun ways. Missing out on time with people is like a small death to Blaise. In seeing this, I learned that Blaise didn't have to be spanked for every major offense. He could be given a time out instead, which could be equally if not more effective.

Every technique that we learned in the research study employed a systematic approach. For example, the process for a time out includes a decision tree where next steps depended on how our son responded to the command to go to time out, how he behaved in time out, etc. If you would like more details about this, feel free to contact me and I will gladly share them.

For the sake of this reading, I just wanted to share one additional detail. Following time out, the interaction with your child needs to be as though nothing ever happened. We were taught to engage them right back into whatever the family is doing. Talk of the offense was to be saved for a later time and the only immediate thing that may need to happen related to the offense is an apology or a clean-up if applicable. However, the child should not be badgered about what happened once the time out is complete. This way, the time out remains in the place where it is taken and does not follow the child wherever she goes. Doing this also contrasts the fun of time with family to the monotony of sitting in time out alone.

This concept was difficult for me to apply but makes so much sense. In the past when my children were defiant, I dwelled on it. My feelings didn't leave after the punishment, they lingered, and I wanted them to know it! But the minute the psychologist explained this practice to us, I thought, *This is just how God is with me. He throws my sins into the sea of forgetfulness and remembers them no more* (Micah 7:19). In leaving that time out on the steps, we teach our children the wonderful power of God's grace.

With our son, Blaise, time out was a go-to punishment for the offenses of destructive behavior, physical aggression towards others, lying, and defiance. These were behaviors that had been strongholds in our son's life, so we reserved this big kahuna of punishments for these actions. If we were to use the time out for every wrong thing he did, he would have become desensitized to it, and it would have been ineffective. That's why incorporating a mix of punishments is essential.

Spanking

One day when I was about 10 years old or so, my dad was about to leave for a jog through the neighborhood. I asked if I could go with him and he told me "no." I didn't like that answer, so I decided to go out to try and find him. As I was looking for him, I came across another man who was jogging. He wasn't at all familiar to me, but he was nice enough. I struck up a conversation and began jogging alongside him.

When we rounded the corner back to my street, who did I see jogging right towards me but my dad. As he neared, I lost step with the jogging man I had picked up, turned, and got in step with my dad. I remember my dad saying as his breathing labored from the exercise, "I told you…to stay inside. Go inside the house…and wait for me there." No spanking was good, but a spanking from Dad was *the* worst. Strangely enough, I remember the circumstances surrounding the spanking, but I don't remember the spanking itself. What I remember the most is thinking, *I will never do that again!* When spanking is done right, this should be a child's take-away:

> *The pain of this punishment is not*
> *worth me doing this again.*

I feel it is vital to be candid about the topic of spanking, so parents no longer fear the repercussions of using corporal punishment with their children. For too long spanking has been a taboo topic, leaving parents without guidance as to how to do it because they are "closet spankers." My hope is that having an open dialogue about the process would promote proper discipline measures and help to prevent the negative consequences commonly associated with spanking.

When spanking our children, we use a wooden spoon (up until about age 6 or 7) or a folded belt (between ages 8-11) on their buttocks. The purpose of spanking on the buttocks is because it's fleshy and will not cause physical harm. However, the hurt should be enough to deter our child from making the same wrong choice.

We use a tool to spank in order to avoid an association with our hands causing them harm. It is natural for a child to have a fearful reaction when he sees a parent approaching him with a spanking spoon in hand. However, he should not have a fearful reaction when he sees a parent's hands reaching for him. This is the reason for using an object as the middleman—we don't want our children to confuse the intentions of Mommy's and Daddy's hands.

In our family, the child's responsibility is to be submissive to the spanking. Certainly not easy for a child to do because the instinct is to protect himself from pain. Speaking of pain, I want to take a moment to share with you that writing about this is difficult. I don't like recalling the pain that my children had to go through because of disobedience. As I share this information with you, my transparency is meant to give you help—not to glorify the measures we use. Just like God, we want our children to get it so that they *don't* need to suffer painful consequences. But when they don't get it, our responsibility is to train them to turn from wrongful behaviors.

Proverbs 22:6 says, *"Start children off on the way they should go, and even when they are old they will not turn from it."*

Imagine a world of adults who were not trained as children. It is very likely that there would be no more world, if this were the case. Training our children in small things while they are still young provides a protective foundation from the bigger things when they are adults.

Training in this manner is shared equally by Ross and me. Typically, we implement spanking with a child who will not submit his or her will to our authority. Our goal is for the child to repent—recognize wrong behavior and then turn away from it. Therefore, we administer the number of spanks necessary for this to happen. Typically, it is two or three. Sometimes it's less, sometimes it's more. As a parent, it is imperative that we seek guidance from Holy Spirit and not our flesh when disciplining in this manner. For this reason, I'm sharing some steps to follow when spanking is the appropriate discipline for your child.

How to Prepare Yourself Before Spanking

1. **Pray.** Ask Holy Spirit to help you use self-control and patience with your child just like God uses self-control and patience in dealing with you.

2. **Send your child ahead of you.** By having your child arrive at the designated spanking area ahead of you, you can compose yourself and put some space between the offense and the punishment.

3. **Talk to your child first.** Before you spank, tell your child what the offense was and what to expect. This helps to connect you to the child and diffuse the emotions related to the offense. Be specific about how

many spanks they are getting. Remember, you are punishing them for what they have done and not for how you feel about what they have done.

There have been times, sadly, when we have had to restrain our children to spank them. I understand that this seems cruel. But even crueler is how they may end up if we do not deliver the discipline that they need. Scripture is clear about this.

A wise son brings joy to his father, but a foolish son brings grief to his mother. Proverbs 10:1

A wise son brings joy to his father, but a foolish man despises his mother. Proverbs 15:20

Whoever robs their father and drives out their mother is a child who brings shame and disgrace. Proverbs 19:26

If someone curses their father or mother, their lamp will be snuffed out in pitch darkness. Proverbs 20:20

Whoever robs their father or his mother and says, "It is not wrong," is partner to one who destroys. Proverbs 28:24

A rod and reprimand impart wisdom, but a child left undisciplined disgraces its mother. Proverbs 29:15

These scriptures reinforce the fact that despite our children's reaction or resistance, appropriate discipline is necessary to keep them on the right path. Below I have included some additional steps to help the resistant child who requires discipline through spanking.

How to Help a Child Who Resists a Spanking

1. Pray. Notice a pattern here? Only God has the power to manage our children's behavior.

2. Don't dialogue. In the case of a resistant child, less is more. Since the child is worked up about the punishment, it is best to administer the punishment as quickly as possible and talk later.

3. No plea bargaining. To help your child, you must not give in to any attempts to get out of the punishment. When you do, you lose the control and they gladly accept it.

4. Quickly and unemotionally subdue the child. As best you can get your child into a position where you can spank their bottom. With a child who resists, it is not easy and I can almost guarantee your emotions will peak. This is where you must go back to #1 and ask for God's help with self-control. Your directive is to administer the spanking in the proper way without doing anything that is driven by the emotions of the moment. Since this is not natural, the help of Holy Spirit is required.

Following a spanking, a child must be restored. This is equivalent to welcoming a child back into family activity after a time out. In this case, restoration should include affection and forgiveness. Hug them and hold them tight. Lead them in asking for forgiveness for their offense. Then **eagerly give forgiveness without exception**. After a spanking, your child should be left with no doubt in his mind that he is loved by you. For an excellent Biblical example of this, see the parable of the lost son in Luke 15:11-32.

As our children grow older, punishments change. Spankings stopped for our older kids around adolescence. This was for several reasons. One reason is that as a child is developing into a young man or woman, having to get a spanking tends to be more embarrassing. Another reason is that there are other punishments that are much more effective with older kids. And finally, when kids get older, punishments should resemble what they will experience in the real world.

I remember our oldest son went upstairs for a spanking from Ross one day for something he had done. I believe he was 13 at the time. It had been quite some time since he had been spanked and I thought to myself, *I wonder how this is going to go.* Moments later, Ross came downstairs and I asked him about it. He said, "I spanked him once on the bottom and we both started laughing. He's too old for this now." Needless to say, this was Hunter's final spanking.

DISCIPLINE FOR OLDER SCHOOL AGE CHILDREN

Loss of Privileges

As our children grew older, certain things began to matter to them a lot more than they once did. Electronic devices, their bedtime, television shows, money, sports, and time with friends each hold a place of value in our kids' lives. When they became valuable to our children is when we began using the removal of them as punishment.

During a faculty in-service at the high school where my husband teaches, a guest speaker referred to the teachers who taught at the school as "technology immigrants" and the children who went to the school as "technology natives." This has always stuck with me, especially as our youngest displays an affinity for cell phones and tablets like babies used to display an affinity for teddy bears and baby dolls. Today's youth intuitively master electronic devices as though this ability is part of their genetic make-up. Just the other day, my son was writing—excuse me—texting a paper for class on his cell phone. When I asked him, "Wouldn't that be a lot easier to do on the computer?" he simply responded, "No because I'm so used to texting anyway." Crazy.

Because these devices are such a big part of our children's lives, their removal can be a very effective punishment as well as a very effective incentive. When I would tell my older kids that I will hold onto their cell phones until they talk with a teacher about a grade, believe you me, they got moving. It saves the energy and frustration that parents feel from yelling at their kids to do things or not to do things. Instead the child shoulders the responsibility and tends to readily take care of business to avoid prolonged time apart from their device.

I would like to take a sidebar from the topic at hand to share briefly about monitoring kids with electronic devices. My husband and I have tried to keep our children off their devices when they shouldn't be on them. We have also tried to keep our children from going onto internet sites that they shouldn't be on. In both cases, we have failed. Just like us, our children are human, and they give in to temptation. Their mistakes, however, can be priceless opportunities to talk about self-control, grace, and so many other life topics.

Once Morgan and Hunter were seniors in high school, they were permitted to have their phones in their room at night instead of leaving them downstairs on the kitchen counter. This transferred responsibility into their hands and out of ours. Certainly, we could've taken the phones and hid them, but this wouldn't teach them self-discipline. We are preparing our teens to live life on their own in the very near future and certainly mom and dad aren't going to be around to hide their phones when they aren't using them properly.

When the rules are broken, we do take their device away for a predetermined amount of time. During this time, sometimes the device is left in plain view and sometimes it is not. However, God has a way of helping us to discover when they are disobedient. We don't even have to dig around for evidence, He makes it very plain. I love it.

Morgan and Hunter did not know our Wi-Fi password. When-ever they wanted to get on the internet, they had to come to us to enter the password. Up until they were several years into high school, once they were finished using the internet, we made them make the device forget the Wi-Fi password before turning it off. This isn't foolproof as there have been many occasions when we have forgotten to oversee them turning off the Wi-Fi. And that's okay. This has allowed for them to make independent decisions as to whether they will do right or wrong. Again, the goal is not simply obedience, but preparation for a future apart from mom and dad. Chapter 7 will go into greater depth surrounding the topic of electronic devices.

Although electronics are a big deal to most kids, there can be equally effective means of punishment. For Blaise there have been times when we have not let him play in a baseball game. This is torture in his eyes. He loves sports and it is an outlet for his energy and athleticism. We have only used this punishment a handful of times because it works so well to straighten out his behavior long-term. At the beginning of the season, we share the possibility of this punishment ahead of time with Blaise's coach. Then again during the season, if he approaches the point of his actions costing him playing time, we warn his coach that the punishment is imminent. Communication with Blaise's coach allows proper preparation time for the team and provides another adult to challenge Blaise in making good choices.

One year during the fall ball season, Blaise had to sit out of two games. We recognized that some parents on our team have a very competitive nature and were not pleased because Blaise is an outstanding baseball player. However, the blessing was that they never said anything to *us* about the consequence, they addressed *Blaise* instead.

On one of the occasions, a mom asked him if he had apologized for what he had done. Another time a dad remarked to him, "Stay out of trouble, Buddy. Your team needs you." During a double-header, where we had made the decision to bench him the first game and allow him to play the second, another mom questioned, "Blaise was what you did worth it?" Whoa. There he was behind the fence watching his teammates battle for a win to play the next game for the championship and she springs that on him. I thought to myself, *Wow, this punishment is better than anything we could have planned.* Oftentimes it's those natural consequences that speak more clearly than any amount of nagging from you.

Removal of time with friends is another punishment that we have used. Now, you can only use it if time with friends is important to your child. Early in our son Hunter's school career, friends were not a hot commodity. He could take them or leave them. Don't get me wrong, he knew how to be friendly, but he didn't have any kids with which he was close. During late middle school, that changed and eventually we would routinely hear about the antics of his buddies at the lunch table or during a track meet.

It used to be that when our children were invited to a party, with a few exceptions, we generally allowed them to attend. Through the research study that we participated in, we now recognize that a party or even going to play outside with a friend can be used as a reward.

During high school, our daughter requested to attend a handful of parties with mixed company. After confirming adequate supervision, we allowed her to attend because of her responsiveness in the following areas: schoolwork, behavior, and helpfulness. These qualities may not get rewarded in the everyday, but they build up her account of faithfulness in our eyes and eventually reward favorable dividends.

During our son Blaise's middle school years, we used a specific reward system where he earned social privileges through his behavior. However, he could also get more immediate rewards like going outside to play with a friend when all his chores were done *well*. Using these opportunities has been a big help in getting him to move quickly, but oftentimes at the expense of thoroughness. Hence, another teaching opportunity, in this instance about the importance of doing work that is worthy of the Lord (Colossians 3:23-24).

In the past, a social privilege within our home was the time that each child went to bed. It was a BIG deal. Not every child had the same bedtime, therefore the loss of time staying up was a strong incentive to do right. Eventually we began using an early bedtime as a logical consequence. A logical consequence is one that is connected to a misbehavior—in other words, it makes sense that this punishment would be linked with this particular behavior.

For example, on occasions when our children have stayed up later than their bedtime, their punishment would be an earlier bedtime the next day that is equivalent to the length of time they stayed up past their bedtime. Or if a younger child refused to take a nap as we've requested, his consequence is an earlier bedtime so that his body gets the rest it needs. Our previous practice had been to dole out punishments that suited our tastes no matter how they related to the behavior at hand. Now we try to follow the rule of letting the punishment fit the crime as best we can. This also serves well in that our children tend to know what to expect in terms of punishment and can think ahead of time about the consequence and potentially self-correct their behavior.

Natural and Logical Consequences: Money and More

The almighty dollar. Throughout history it has been a powerful motivator. The Bible tells us that the love of money is the root of all kinds of evil and that some eager for it have wandered from the faith and pierced themselves with many griefs (1 Timothy 6:10). Money in and of itself isn't evil, but when we put its importance in a place before God and before others, evil is birthed.

I have shared my personal account of life lessons with money in *Personal Finances Personal Freedom*. In that book, I also share about how we've been teaching our children from a young age how to manage money with the hopes of them avoiding the mishaps we encountered. Now, I intend to share with you how we use money to influence our children's behavior.

Our third child, Blaise, is a giver. He gets joy out of giving to others. He doesn't necessarily keep track of birthdays and holidays to plan ahead of time, but you better believe if he finds out it's Father's Day or someone's birthday, he will disappear into the basement, gather some materials, and put together something honoring the individual. I'm smiling right now thinking about the time he's used a thank you card as a birthday card during one of his spur-of-the-moment crafting sessions. It truly is a blessing to see his thoughtfulness in action. I feel as though the phrase, *It's the thought that counts*, was penned with Blaise in mind.

Just as much as Blaise is a giver, he is also a spender. This makes sense because, if he enjoys giving to others, that includes any retailer who is ready and willing to take his money. As you can imagine or may have already experienced, it can be challenging to convince a spender not to spend. *"It's my money." "It doesn't cost that much." "I deserve this."* To this day, we make it a point to slow Blaise down when it comes to spending. It may come in the form of having him leave a potential purchase behind at a store and consider it overnight. Sometimes we have him shop around to look for other options. And other times we simply say "no" because we realize that it is not a good decision for him.

As kids, Morgan and Hunter also enjoyed spending money, but they also had more of a capacity to think ahead to the future, realizing that they needed to save money. For example, they both paid for their cell phone plans. Knowing this, they purposely withheld from spending all their money to plan for what was coming up. As a parent, I was thrilled at their understanding of the concept that not all money is spending money.

As I talked about earlier, since money is of value to our kids, it can be an effective punishment. One time, Blaise had a temper tantrum and did some damage to our stairs. In addition to getting a time out (consequence for destructive behavior) he also had to pay for the parts at the hardware store to fix the stair railing. Conversely, a few bucks have been a reward for that same child for a successful week in his behavior program. In both instances, money has served as an effective motivator to do the right thing.

There is one instance of a natural consequence with money in our family I will never forget. It was Christmas time and we were away visiting my in-loves. They had given each of us (Ross, the kids, and me) $100 as a gift. The next day when we went shopping, we split up—Ross was with the boys and I was with Morgan. Our plan was to meet up in the middle of the mall at a set time. Morgan and I were a little late and the guys were already there. Looking at their faces from a distance, I could tell that something had happened. Ross looked annoyed, Blaise's eyebrows were furrowed, and Hunter...well, Hunter just looked like Hunter.

"What's the matter?" I asked.

"Blaise lost his money," Ross announced, clearly ticked.

I took a deep breath. I wanted to console my son. I wanted to console Ross.

Before I could say anything else, Ross recounted the story of the last place he knew Blaise had the money, where they had looked, and the lecturing he had already given to Blaise. It sounded like all bases had been covered. We talked together about possible other options and once those were exhausted, we headed out to leave.

Upon getting settled inside the van, Blaise piped up in a desperate voice, "What money am I going to use to shop now?"

"I don't know," Ross retorted, still clearly irritated at Blaise's lack of responsibility and stubbornness in not letting him hold onto his money in the first place.

I decided to address Morgan and Hunter. "Guys, your brother lost his money in the mall. We've let people know about it, but we don't know if he's going to get it back. I am asking if each of you would be willing to give Blaise $20. Please know that it is up to you. You don't have to do it."

Without delay their responses came, "I'll do it."

"Sure, he can have $20. That still leaves me with $80."

No negativity whatsoever came through in their responses. My husband also gave $20 to Blaise. So, despite the circumstances, along with my $20, each of us still had $80 left. This started out as a natural consequence. *You lost $100. Oh well. Maybe you'll do things a little differently next time around.* But God didn't leave it that way. He used it to show an awesome demonstration of how gracious He is with us when the stakes are high. When we make big, costly mistakes, He still gives us another chance and loves us through our mess ups.

Natural and logical consequences can certainly be utilized beyond the arena of money. It's simply a matter of:

1. Letting the consequences of poor choices play out (natural consequences)

Or

2. Deciding on a consequence that suits the offense (logical consequences)

One hot summer day our family was driving home from somewhere. Two of the kids had been arguing the latter part of the ride home to the point where it was unbearable. Ross stopped at the bottom of the hill that leads up to our development, opened the sliding door on the van, and told the kids, "Get out! I'm sick of the arguing. You're walking home." They got out, the door slid shut behind them, and we went on our way as they endured the scorching, sticky walk up the hill. They were too parched by the time they reached home to continue any arguing.

On another occasion our son, Blaise, had been misbehaving on the bus to the point of getting suspended from the bus for a time. Whenever this happens, we add additional days to his suspension because he LOVES riding the bus and we want him to realize that it is a privilege he needs to take seriously. The other thing that we do is have him pay us gas money for taking him to and from school since he has temporarily forfeited his free transportation. (The kids also pay us gas money if they miss their bus in the morning. We do give them grace on a case by case basis.)

A friend from church suggested having him walk to school, which wasn't possible because of him being too young.

"How far can he safely walk to school?" the friend inquired.

"Down the hill to the plaza below our development," I responded.

"Have him do that then."

For the entire week that Blaise wasn't allowed to take the bus, he had to walk from our home down to the plaza at the bottom of the hill (the same hill the kids had to walk up on that hot day). He also had to walk from the bottom of the hill up to our home after school each day. He was only in 3rd grade at that point, so as he walked, I watched him from certain checkpoints to keep an eye on him. He didn't seem too phased by this consequence until one morning when there was a downpour. Not only was it raining, it was cold, and the wind was blowing every which way. I remember his frowning face.

"It's raining," he told me. "

Yes, I know," I answered.

"What am I gonna do?" he asked.

"You're going to walk." I gave him a little poncho to wear and started driving.

At one of the checkpoints he came up and started pounding on the van, "Let me in! I'm cold! I wanna get in!"

I wound the window down just enough to tell him in a stern voice, "Back away from the van so I can drive." He shouted at me a little longer and after realizing that he was not getting anywhere but wet, he backed away, and I moved on to the next checkpoint.

Whenever possible, I strongly encourage you to implement natural and logical consequences as the lessons learned through this method of discipline are invaluable and memorable. Nevertheless, each form of discipline has a time and place. As you hear from the Lord and grow to know your child, you can determine which one is most appropriate to foster obedience.

Chapter 6

BE A FAN

O ne of my biggest joys as a mom has been to encourage and support my children in whatever is of interest to them. Our oldest son Hunter presented us with the most opportunities with which to practice.

It started when he was around 2 or 3 and my in-loves purchased a train set for him. It was pretty basic, with one train and a track that went in a circle and up a hill. Well, that put Hunter on a train kick, and he was into everything about trains. We checked out train books at the library, we visited several places where trains were on display or making runs, and that simple train set morphed into multiple bins of track, engines, train cars, and various other train accessories.

Next, he fell in love with tractor trailer trucks. He read books about them, identified them as we drove down the highway, and even had a birthday party where he and a few of his friends got a ride through our neighborhood in the cab of our neighbor's semi-truck. (I'll forever remember the fear that gripped me sitting in the passenger seat as we lurched forward to start the ride and his then baby brother just missed flying head first onto the floor of the cab.) Then came Legos. After that it was cars (but only the cars that Mom and Dad cannot afford), and now finally music and music production. During each of these phases, I have sought out whatever resources I could to encourage his interest.

In 2 Timothy 1:6, Paul tells Timothy to fan into flame the gift of God that is inside of him. He was speaking about the gift of faith that Timothy had as did his mother and grandmother. Each of our children also have gifts. If they are believers in Jesus Christ, they have spiritual gifts. However, God has also given them talents, abilities, and interests that are specific to what they are to be doing in His Kingdom. In the Bible, Dorcas possessed the ability to make clothing, and God used her talent to provide for widows. David was talented in music, and God used him to calm King Saul's spirit. Jewish leaders interested in Jesus' teachings handled the precious task of laying our Savior's body to rest. The obsessions, quirks, and interests that our children have inside of them are to be used outside of them for the glory of God. Nothing is wasted.

Our son, Blaise, has changed our lives forever. We could not parent him like we did our older kids when they were his age. He has required a whole new set of directives. Our parenting style for Morgan and Hunter was like reading Chinese instructions to him—it didn't translate at all. But a place where he could shine and receive accolades has always been athletics. He has a natural inclination for sports that his older brother and sister do not have. Out on a field he's on task, comfortable, successful, and satisfied. It's something he's been made to do well. As the athletic fields level life's playing field for Blaise, we can see him in a different light and celebrate his talent by being his biggest fans.

Given the major differences between our children, it can be difficult to not compare our kids to one another and especially to other kids. There have been times when our hearts have ached upon seeing the accomplishments of another child.

That could have been Morgan if she had worked harder.

Look what Hunter missed out on because he didn't take that opportunity.

Blaise could be an even better pitcher if he would learn to take instruction.

I wish Story was going to the potty like Sammy.

Sound familiar? I know it's familiar to somebody because not only do I myself think these thoughts, I hear parents saying them to others—and to their children. I have made this mistake on more than one occasion. Certainly, as parents we have a responsibility to encourage our kids to do everything heartily as unto the Lord. But after the encouragement, we need to put the matter into His hands and trust that the outcome will be what He intends.

Remember how we talked about natural consequences in Chapter 5. This is one of those instances where they can be used to teach the lesson better than we can. When your child sees the accolades of a peer or a sibling, it affects them. They may act as though they don't care, but don't adults do the same thing? We are prideful beings and we don't want people knowing when we're hurt or disappointed. Trust me, or better yet trust God, that they are getting the message. While we wait on them to grow in understanding, we can pray and not let our disappointment get in the way of their learning.

Along with our children's phenomenal talents come some astronomical costs. Lessons, organized sports, classes, equipment, and the like can take a toll on the family budget. Many families plunge into these activities and consider the costs later. It can be an expensive undertaking that should not be taken lightly.

As much as possible, we have made a point of having our children contribute towards the cost of their activities. Since our kids get an allowance, they can pay for them little by little. Once the oldest two had jobs, they often paid for their share in full and sometimes chose to cover the cost completely. In doing so, they are investing in themselves. I value that in which I invest because obtaining it takes time and sacrifice. Our desire is that our kids would share that same sentiment.

The scale that we use for the contribution our kids make towards an activity expense is below:

$150 & up=pay 25%
$75-$149=pay 30%
$11-$74=pay 35%
$10 & under=pay 100%

Putting a price tag on activities also serves to give our kids some pause as they consider, "Hmm, is it worth that much to me?" Certainly, as parents, we have the final say regarding the commitment our family can make in other regards such as time and priorities. But incorporating conversation around financial commitment is good practice for them in helping to make wise future choices.

Because we've been blessed with exactly 2.1 more children than the average U.S. household, we need to be cognizant of the multiple directions in which life tugs at us. With each child comes a potential activity or activities and those are multiplied by 4 different young people usually with entirely different interests. When our kids were little, we would actively seek out activities to engage them in. It was fun testing out a sport or an instrument, always anticipating a Webb phenom. But soon enough we were attempting to throw away any sports/camp/music/club flyers that came home in the kids' backpacks before they even could lay eyes on them. Okay, I, not Ross, was the one trying to throw them away. It unnerved me that with each potential activity came a pull in another direction. And when you're pulled in so many directions, how can one ever be in one place? How can one rest?

Although I'm more of the barometer for this, Ross and I both recognized early on the need to limit time given to our children's pursuits. We've tried to stick to permitting the kids to be involved in only one activity at a time that runs outside of school hours. Sometimes it was just a matter of logistics. With only two of us and more than two of them, we had to run a zone defense—not everyone could be covered. Also, we wanted to be able to participate as a family in each child's events. Following this practice, it has been doable. Typically, we are available to attend the concert, celebration, performance, or ceremony of each child as a family.

As you can probably tell, I'm a firm believer that more time needs to be spent in the home than away from it (more on this in Chapter 7). I know it's common for families to be on the go more than on the stay. But just because it's common doesn't mean it is best. Home is the training ground for these little astronauts who are going to be orbiting the world on their own one day. Yes, they can and do learn great lessons from involvement in activities outside the home. But we have been assigned as their mission control leaders. For this reason, it is imperative that we don't neglect spending ample amounts of time with them.

Once the activities come along, it can be difficult for a child to remember that their main directive is to get a good education. When they engage in an activity and especially when they are good at it, it can be difficult as a parent to remember this directive, too. Let me go one step further to say that it can be difficult even when your child is *not good* at their choice activity. Whether it's marching band, recreational baseball, or boy scouts, the activity extends into a community—almost like a church. You share the common bond of your children being in the group. You help and share with one another. You even eat with one another at group picnics and celebrations.

Essentially, you become a family. No one likes to disappoint family. Thus, we say yes to our children participating in later practices, extra practices, and special subgroups that pull time away from study and home life. We readily volunteer our time as booster officers, food preparers, costume room attendants, and den leaders to give back to the groups that are enriching our children's lives. Herein lies the catch 22 of the one night of the week that Johnny doesn't have football practice, mom is out for the night chairing the booster club meeting. Opportunity is lost for the whole family to have time together.

As parents, we set the standard for our children's priorities. If we regularly miss church for a child's activities, we are sending a message. If we set limits on our engagement in a child's activity so that we do not miss church regularly, we are sending a message. Which message will you send? The same goes for allowing our children to participate in an activity when they are not performing their best in school. (Notice I didn't say when they don't have all A's and B's. Children are so different that their grade is not always a true indicator of their performance.) It is imperative that we as parents lead our kids in showing them how to put first things first. When we do this in our own lives, they'll pick up on it and do it for themselves.

At the time of this writing, our daughter Morgan is leaving to go to college in a little over a month. She has picked up extra hours at her job to pay for additional expenses. When asked about availability, she intentionally requested to be off Sundays all day and Wednesday evenings. Why? Because that's when we attend Sunday worship and Wednesday night Bible study. In our own lives, Ross and I have set limits on activities that we allow to intersect those key times. Morgan followed suit. Our second child, Hunter, who at this time is at a crossroads in his faith in Jesus, even still restricted himself from working during those times. The example that you set in your household matters.

When done correctly, actively engaging in an extra-curricular community can be a tremendous opportunity to share our faith. A specific instance comes to my mind. A parent from our son's recreational baseball team is quite the talker and very frank. I remember being exposed to her for the first time during one of the games and thinking, *I wouldn't want to be on that woman's bad side.*

Well, after some time she began "pecking" at me, in other words, trying to see what I was all about. We had never met before because our kids attend different schools. It was as if she wanted to know me without saying she wanted to know me. I, on the other hand, just wanted to stay as far away from her as possible. Oblivious of my feelings, she began engaging me by teasing—gauging my response and seeing how far she could go.

One of the things she would tease me about was that every time Ross would arrive to a game or leave, he would give me a kiss on the lips. As I said earlier, it's something we've done for years. Whenever one of us comes or goes we kiss. She picked up on this and would even go so far as to announce what was about to happen when she'd see Ross coming onto the premises. "Oh, here comes her man, everybody. He's gonna lay one right smack on her lips as soon as he comes over." Sure enough, her play by play was true every time. But little by little I became less annoyed with it. Instead I started thinking that if it stood out that much to her, that's good. You know, the whole salt and light thing? (Matthew 5:13-16)

So I began to relax about being in the spotlight and instead just let it ride. Over time it became evident that I was a Christian and that triggered her to sarcastically add the tag line "Please pray for me, Chanty" after every crass remark or curse word she let come out of her mouth. But ultimately today we have a friendship of mutual respect and I enjoy her company. (It's funny because without even realizing I was going to write this, I just ran into this very woman today after not seeing her for almost a year.) It is these types of relationships, grown through time and circumstance, that God can use to bring people to Him.

Another light that we let shine is that of the requirement of obedience from our children. Our baller Blaise, as noted earlier, has sat out of games and/or missed practices more times than he would have liked due to poor choices. On one occasion we did not allow him to play on the summer all-star team. He would have easily qualified for the team because he is an outstanding player. However, our prerequisites at home for making the all-star team are not limited to all-star ability, but also include an all-star attitude.

He was devastated. We were disappointed, too. We absolutely love seeing Blaise do what he seems made to do. But more important is the shaping of this young man's heart. A few summers ago we attended a party hosted by the family of one of Blaise's past teammates. The husband was talking to Ross and me about his frustrations with how his son's head coach handled discipline issues on the team. He said that if he was head coach, many of the kids would be sitting the bench for their attitudes and actions. Then he said, "That's why I really appreciate how you guys don't let Blaise play when he's not doing right. Kids need to be held accountable for their actions." His words sailed through my soul like a home run. What a joy to hear someone affirming and understanding what you're doing—making difficult investments in the present for a glorious payoff in the future.

Chapter 7

I SCREEN, YOU SCREEN, WE ALL SCREEN...

Behold the glorious blue-light based hue that glows forth! Calling me, calling you, calling our children to see what lies in wait. No longer are digital devices a rite of passage for teenagers. In this day and age, we frequently spot them clenched in the chubby hands of toddlers and premeditatedly propped up in front of infants to view their contents.

If you could talk with my children regarding my view on digital devices, you would likely come away thinking that I am a screen vigilante. Yet I really do enjoy the conveniences that devices, especially my phone, provide. I love being able to quickly look up something on my phone instead of waiting for my laptop to power up. I'd be lost without my digital calendar that allows me to plug in a reminder the instant it comes to mind. And don't get me started on my affinity for "spoken texts" that let me quickly communicate with someone instead of taking minutes to text with my index finger. But I really feel that much of the communication these devices were supposed to enhance has been highly overrated. Yes, the quantity of communication has increased. Just looking at the sum total of your tween's or teen's text messages will validate this fact. However, in exchange, the quality of communication has dwindled.

When texting first became big, I held out for a couple of years before engaging. Why? Well for one thing, it was not included on our phone plan so whenever I sent or received a text it was at an additional cost. But more importantly, I didn't like feeling that someone couldn't be bothered with talking to me or that I couldn't be bothered talking with them. It seemed the message was, "I'm thinking of you but don't have it in me to invest in a conversation with you right now."

I feel that through texting some basic skills are lost. Namely, the art of tactful, direct communication. We lose opportunities to practice our manners, our assertiveness, and even our tone of voice. Text messages allow us to communicate tone with emojis so much so that we can convey a smile when we're not even smiling. And other times our tone is totally miscommunicated because on the receiving end of that text—it's just words.

I eventually did begin texting because of my pastor. Every once and a while he would say to me, "Chanty, did you get my text?" "No, I don't have texting, Pastor," I'd remind him. "Oh, I sent you something the other day. I'll have to see if I can email it to you." Well, after about five or so conversations like that, I decided to start texting. At that point, we had already added it on to our plan for Ross, so it didn't cost any extra. Now after several years, I must admit I really enjoy the convenience of it. I can send information quickly. I can keep in contact with the folks younger than me who pretty much text in place of talking. And best of all, I can send pictures of the kids to my in-loves who live a distance away. Texting is akin to Facebook for me. I'm not on Facebook at this time, but nonetheless I make sure those who want to know what's going on with us stay updated by texting pictures to them.

One of the many conversations we've had to have with our kids, regarding use of digital devices, is when to have a verbal conversation versus sending a text message. Because they rely so heavily on texting to communicate with their peers, it's mistakenly thought that this form of communication is adequate for everyone. Quite honestly, adults have also been known to rely on texting as a crutch to avoid confrontational situations. We train our kids to make phone calls when situations involve explanation, especially when a certain tone needs to be conveyed. They know that an apology without question requires a phone call or, when feasible, a face-to-face conversation. As believers, we cannot allow the technology of the world to replace the theology of God's Kingdom. Matthew 5:23-24 reads,

Therefore, if you are offering your gift at the altar and there remember that your brother or sister has something against you, leave your gift there in front of the altar. First go and be reconciled to them; then come and offer your gift.

Go. Not text. Not tweet. And for the love of God, not message on Facebook! Go! There is something in the going. It takes consideration. It takes time. It takes humility.

And once you're there, the words, "Please forgive me," are simply a formality. You've already sacrificed much to "go" and the person whom you've offended should see that plainly.

Morgan and Hunter did not have a digital device until they were 11 and 12 or maybe 10 and 11—somewhere in that range. My in-loves asked us if they could buy them each a Kindle for Christmas. Ross and I considered it thoroughly. We understood the draw these devices have on old and young minds alike. For the longest time our kids had been begging us for something, *anything*, electronic. We didn't have any video game consoles. We had a TV but no cable. At the time they didn't have cell phones. We had a PC which they got some entertainment from, but it was used primarily for our needs.

After some discussion, we decided to let them have the devices. Blaise, who would have been around 6 or 7 at the time, got a Leapfrog tablet. Yet Story was introduced to Blaise's old Leapfrog tablet at around 3 years of age. And Blaise got a Kindle for Christmas when he was around 8 years old. Doesn't sound fair, does it? Well, in our home we don't do what's fair, we do what we believe to be right. With our older kids, we really felt the burden of setting a standard in our household of putting first things first. Schoolwork is a kid's job. We didn't want schoolwork playing second fiddle to entertainment. Morgan and Hunter had a natural affinity for books. They both became voracious readers at a very young age. I can still remember Hunter telling me the story from one of his books and me realizing that I had never read that book to him. He was reading, and he was probably only about 3 years old. I believe that his environment helped to sway him in this direction. Once our younger two children came along, they had two older siblings through which to see the standard lived out. We could introduce electronics sooner without there being any confusion as to our family's priorities.

Additionally, not every kid is ready for everything at the same time. As parents, it's our job to read our kids and know what's appropriate for them—what's going to help them to be their very best. For some kids, because of how they learn, digital devices enhance their abilities and spur them onto success. For other kids these devices are a distraction and may cause learning to be stunted. Readiness also includes financial readiness. Morgan wanted a phone since she was in middle school, but never put aside the money to buy one or to finance a monthly plan for one (both requirements for having a phone in the Webb household). Hunter, at about age 13, saved up money for a phone and a phone plan, all before having a steady job. After approving him having a phone and seeing that he had prepared for the expenses, we okayed the purchase.

Just to be clear, preparation in the beginning does not always mean responsibility in the end. Both of our kids strayed once given the freedom of a phone. By straying, I mean looking at inappropriate digital content, breaking phone usage rules, texting with foul language, and accessing content through unlawful means. Sounds bad, huh? But if I look at my life as an adult, I can say that I have done the same whether through my phone or through other means. How about you? The point is, even though they own their phones, we own our kids, and Jesus owns us. Their iPhones came at a price (except for the hand-me-down ones from Grandma) and we were bought at a price. God places value on us and we place value on our children. We're not going to step aside and let our valuables go just anywhere or say just anything. No. There's a standard. It's found in the Bible. We're told in Philippians 4:8, *"…whatever is true, whatever is noble, whatever is right, whatever is pure, whatever is lovely, whatever is admirable—if anything is excellent or praiseworthy—think about such things."* As Christ-following parents, we have an obligation to enforce this principle in our children's lives, especially their digital lives.

Think about it. When we allow our children to have free reign of their digital devices, we are not drawing a line in the sand where their authority ends and ours begins. As parents, yes, we loosen the leash and provide more opportunity for increased responsibility. But to completely untether a child, not requiring any checks and balances in their life, is a recipe for rebellion. You will likely get pushback from checking browser history, installing parental controls, checking text messages, and taking away digital device privileges. Believe me, we do. Our kids have expressed that they are the only kids they know without free reign of the internet or rights to their devices whenever they see fit. Although this is an exaggeration, sometimes it seemed to be true.

In 1 Kings 19, Elijah is having a pity party because he feels alone in his situation. He's trying to stay faithful but he's being persecuted for it—terrorized and isolated. He's ready to die—and that's just what he tells God. Later in the chapter God speaks to him to let him know that there are thousands strong who are still following Him. It's just that Elijah didn't know about them. This may seem like a dramatic comparison, but in a teenage brain it's spot on. Without a phone they feel alone, disconnected—like they are the only one in their circumstance. Today's kids are so digitally connected that they feel disconnected without that connection.

"What?! No Wi-Fi?"

"What?! I can't have my phone?"

"What?! You wanna talk?"

That is why your role is KEY. They don't know what they really need, and it is our job to teach them. Anyone can give them what they want. The world would love to give them what they want. But who's going to give them the hard things—the things they don't want but need? You and me. Their parents.

We are friends with a couple whose son is like ours in that he learns his lessons the hard way. The wife once joked with me that months earlier his aunt bought him a phone, but he hadn't even had the chance to use it because of his poor choices. I consider these parents one of the many whose knees have not bowed down to Baal. (Read all of 1 Kings 19 to understand the reference.) Just as our teens feel alone in this battle, I feel alone, too. It's not easy saying no with so many other parents saying yes, and my kids looking at me like I'm crazy because I'm in the minority, or often the only one. I've also heard, "But their parents are Christians and they let them…" In some cases, the parents are Christians not making Biblical choices. And in other cases, the parents are Christians, but for our kid and for our family we've decided another choice is best. Again, not fair, but right.

Up until a certain age (depending on the child) we would monitor them whenever they were on the Internet. One of us would be right next to them for the time that they were allotted to be on their device. Just as with learning to ride a bike, more supervision is required to enter this uncharted territory. Then, as time goes on and trust is built, we moved on to allowing them to be on the Internet in a communal area (kitchen, living room) and we would check in on them every so often. Later, the trust builds to the point of letting our children primarily supervise one another on the Internet. I had asked the older two at one point to remind themselves of appropriate internet boundaries by saying, "Check" aloud at which point they would each look at the other's screen. We later moved to the point of allowing our teens to be on the Internet solo in a communal space, and then finally completely at their own discretion.

One additional measure of protection our family decided to implement is a service called *Covenant Eyes*. By subscribing to the service, we receive a report of our children's internet usage by device. So even though they can do whatever they want on the Internet, they will be held accountable when we see the report. Ross subscribed to the service initially and has an accountability partner who receives his reports and follows up with him. Our children's reports come to us and we discuss them with our children as the need arises.

It would be wonderful if once they are out on their own they decide to use the service and implement an accountability partner. Prayerfully, our training helps them to see that it is okay to need help in this and other areas of their lives. I mentioned earlier about the draw that digital tech can have on us as human beings. The affinity that we have towards it can easily morph into full-blown addiction. I've read about it. Seen it in our household. It ain't pretty.

The content on our phones, tablets, and computers are designed to addict us. Don't believe me? Consider slot machines. You pull the handle. A few coins fall out. You pull the handle again. More coins fall out. So, you pull the handle again expecting even more coins to fall out. The same amount of coins falls out as the first time. Yet you still pull the handle because you're at least getting *something* out with the hopes of getting more. The question is, how much are you willing to put in to get something out?

The same goes for our devices. The "pull to refresh" feature used in many apps is the slot machine handle. Users continue to pull, expecting something—something exciting. But eventually we pull to refresh expecting anything. Our bodies and minds create responses based on the satisfaction we previously experienced. We got something before, and we want something again and AGAIN. This is the addictive nature taking control.

One of the best helps we can give our children is to be examples of how to responsibly use our devices: Like putting them down when someone (including our child) is talking to us. Keeping them out of our rooms when it's time to sleep. Having phone "no-zones" like the kitchen table where phones are not allowed. Using only one screen at a time (no TV and tablet). Setting limits on the time we spend on them. These disciplines lived out in our lives serve both us and our children. I am by no means an expert on this topic and I don't live out these disciplines to a "t". However, I'm daily working to set a positive example for my kids of how to responsibly engage with digital tech.

Chapter 8

IS ANYBODY HOME?

Home life is vitally important to me. On Sunday evenings when Ross and I look at our calendar to determine what the upcoming week looks like, I feel that my duty is to safeguard as many evenings as possible at home together as a family.

A key component of any time we spend at home is having dinner together. Sitting at a table during a meal requires a closeness in proximity which yields a closeness in relationship. Speaker and author Devi Titus shares, with amazing insight, the importance of family meal time in a message entitled "The Table Principle." Anytime I am tempted to give the kids dinner without Ross because he's running late, Devi's message goes through my mind. She speaks of the history of the table—both the table we eat at as well as the Bread of the Presence table in the Tabernacle of Biblical times. She specifies how the dimensions and layout of a table foster humanity and connectedness. One cannot sit at a table with another and not be affected in some way. No matter how few or how many are in attendance, our family has made it a practice to eat meals at the table in our home.

Being more present at home allows us to care for the home. Even when I was a homemaker, I was not the sole caretaker. This task belongs to all its occupants starting with Ross on down to Story. It was tempting for me to feel the weight of the responsibility of housekeeping resting solely on my shoulders. After all, I was in the house for the better part of the day. However, our family knows that we all share in the work required to keep up the house.

The responsibility of chores began for our children as soon as they understood the words *clean up*. When they are young, children delight in being helpful because they enjoy the praise (reward) that is lavished on them as a result. As they become older, there is not so much enjoyment on their end and not so much praise on our end. Chores change into duties that just need to be done. Although it's not the norm to praise older kids for doing their chores, I try my best to do just that.

During my ten plus years away from the workforce, I spent much more time inside my home. While there, I was subject to the living conditions of the home. Seeing a sink full of dishes that our daughter didn't have time to do or smelling a cat litter box that our son didn't clean out gave me a whole new appreciation for when the chores are done. There were occasions when I hosted visitors and had to scurry around the house beforehand to pick up stray belongings. These times come to mind when the kids are routinely handling their responsibilities and I try my best to say, "Thank you for emptying out the dishwasher" or whatever other task they may have done to make life more convenient for me. Also, with having a little guy around, the older kids regularly hear and join in on the praise we give to him for cleaning up or being a helper around the house. The consistent praise we give to Story also reminds me that we still need to praise Morgan, Hunter, and Blaise for all that they do on a regular basis to contribute to our household's needs.

A quick example of a chore that we all pitch in to help with is the dishes. When Morgan and Hunter were old enough to handle it, we divided up the responsibility of setting and clearing the table between them. Morgan took odd days and Hunter took even days. As they grew in ability, their responsibility grew into washing dishes as well. Once Blaise became old enough to help, he got thrown into the mix. He is responsible for dish duty on dates that are divisible by three (i.e. 3rd, 6th, 24th, 30th, etc.) The basic sentiment is this—we all eat on dishes, therefore we all clean dishes.

One day I went to the bank to get out my monthly allotment of cash. This includes the kids' allowance which requires coins. As the teller was preparing the money for me, she spoke of how the change reminded her of when she used to pay her kids for doing their chores.

"During the summer my kids loved to go to the pool," she shared. "I would always have a list of chores on a bulletin board that hung beside the steps. Each chore had a monetary value to it depending on the effort it required. The more effort, the more money it was worth. Each of my four kids had to do at least two jobs before we could all go to the pool. Some kids picked the easy ones to get it done and some would compete to be the first to pick the harder ones to earn more money. Either way there was something for everybody to do, even down to my littlest guy. And best of all the work got done."

When I heard this woman's approach I thought, *She needs to be the CEO of something!* What an ingenious plan! First, she provided her kids with several motivators—going to the pool, earning money, and for some of them, earning the *most* money. Then she used positive peer pressure so that she didn't have to nag. *No one* goes to the pool until *everyone* does their chores. Different approach than ours, but successful nonetheless with everyone contributing to the cause. I love it!

Along these same lines, we have often motivated our kids to get chores done by providing an incentive. Like the bank teller, the incentive doesn't have to be something out of the ordinary or cost extra money. Often it is an everyday activity or something you were going to do in the first place. But mentioning that it will be done when chores are finished tends to speed along the process.

For example, before Story was talking, he would grab his shoes and bring them to us, signaling that he wanted to go outside. We responded as follows, "You can go outside after you clean up your books," to which he answered by eagerly going over to pick up his books. With Blaise there would be a knock at our door from a friend asking if he could come outside to play. We would respond, "Blaise still has homework to do. He can come outside after his homework is done." Blaise would overhear and dive into the very homework that he was slow in completing just minutes earlier. The very thing that motivates your child can easily be used to get them to attend to their responsibilities.

Children learn to do chores when they are provided with the opportunity to do them. This statement seems like a no-brainer, but it is easier said than done. Can you recall a time when your child tried to help you make dinner and you took away the mixing spoon sending him on his way before he made a mess? Or when your daughter joined you out in the driveway to shovel snow, but you sent her in because it was too cold? I know I have been guilty of shooing my kids away, especially when they were small, so that I could get my tasks done quickly and without the mess that sometimes accompanies a child's efforts. I was sadly mistaken. Think about it—when your kids become interested in using the potty, you don't keep them from using it. Instead you use their interest to potty-train them. In the same way, as kids become interested in helping with chores, it is prime time to train them.

"Chanty, I am busy. I don't have all kinds of extra time to spend teaching my kids to cook and clean."

Neither do I! But you can use a few minutes of the time you do have allowing your child to help with something you're already doing. Using the potty example again, a child will not sit very long on the potty, even when they say they want to use it. In the same way, a young child will not likely have a sustained attention span to a task that you are doing. You simply engage with them during their period of interest and then finish the task to completion on your own. They will continue learning as they watch you.

Our son Story loved to use the broom whenever he would see me sweeping. As soon as I began sweeping, he would whine and hold his hand up to grasp it from me.

I started playing a game with him so that he could learn to sweep, and so that I could get my work done. I sweep first, and I say, "Mommy's turn!" Then I hand it to him saying, "Story's turn!" We go back and forth until I get my work done. All the while I praise him for being a good helper and work to keep his broom sweeps away from my piles of debris. Yes, it is more time-consuming then if I were to play a video on my phone for him while I whiz through my work. However, the extra effort to teach him means one day *my* work will be *his* work. ☺

Cooking is another task that takes a burden off parents the sooner kids can learn it. All three of our older kids can use the stovetop and oven to cook themselves a meal when necessary. Our oldest son had an egg fetish and learned to cook dippy eggs and omelets when he was around 8 years old. His brother Blaise followed in his footsteps and some mornings can be found with *The Joy of Cooking* opened before him on the kitchen table as he prepares a breakfast dish. We count it a privilege to be able to tell our kids to cook this or that for dinner whenever we go out or go away and know that they can do it. Again, they showed the interest and we provided the opportunity.

Our three older children have been responsible for doing their laundry from an early age. Blaise probably started when he was about 8. I taught him because he was asking to do it. He saw his older brother and sister doing laundry and thought it looked like fun. Ask him what he thinks now! Early on he helped by pouring in the laundry detergent and throwing clothes into the washer as though he were making baskets into a basketball hoop.

Then I showed him how to sort the laundry into piles by colors. We had purchased netted laundry bags for the kids when they first started doing laundry. This eliminated the impossible task of carrying a cumbersome basket down two flights of steps—they just pushed their bags down the steps. Eventually, Blaise was off and running, doing laundry on his own. Until this writing, I have forgotten about the laborious task of laundry in the Webb household. Boy am I thankful to only have the responsibility of laundry for three and not six!

Learning various home responsibilities has taught our children responsibility in serving and gradually led to an income working outside of the home. It began with our daughter Morgan. Not only would she help to look after her younger brother Blaise, she also served monthly as a babysitter for a young adult group in our church. Eventually she decided to take a babysitting course and began a little business called "Rainbow Sitter" where her clients have ranged from babies to doggies. Hunter was next in line with the entrepreneurial spirit. When the boys reach a capable age, Ross will have them help him with maintenance duties around the church. Through this training, Hunter has learned to do tasks like assembling furniture, landscaping, and other odd jobs. Since that time, Hunter has earned money using the very skills that he learned by selflessly serving. Again, I say, it all begins with providing the opportunity.

So certainly, we don't just eat and work at home. The Webbs enjoy entertainment as much as the next family. We especially like to watch movies. Regularly, we would get movies from Redbox since there was a kiosk right down the street (which should make it a breeze to return on time, right? Wrong! Sorry, I will refrain from my Redbox rant.). However, an additional source that I love to use for movies is the local library.

First off, all movies at our library are now **FREE**! I love that word. You can rent a movie for a week and even renew it if no one else is requesting it. Sweet! I like going to the library for movies because sometimes I want to show the kids an oldie but goodie movie from back in my day that I know is clean. Prior to the library making all movies free, I would frequent their collection of movies that were provided free of charge because of their genre. Documentaries, certain cable network series, religious, and informational DVDs are some examples. Not only is there something for everyone, but it gives me the opportunity to expose our kids to some history and information that they might not otherwise encounter. They never know what mom is going to bring home.

Board games were also instrumental for family entertainment. In our previous home, the basement boasted a portable shelving unit filled with board games, in addition to those piled up on the floor next to the shelves. Playing games is a means to communication as well as entertainment. The kids appreciate the level playing field that competition provides, especially when playing a game of chance. For 90 minutes or so, Mom and Dad aren't an authority, but an opponent over whom they might achieve victory. These days it is very seldom that our children break out a board game. More commonly they will play a game solo on an electronic device. Or Ross may pull up a YouTube video he wants to show us. Family entertainment has certainly changed over the years, but what remains the same is the necessity for time together.

We enjoy spending time together outside the home as well. Attending church together, supporting one another's endeavors, or just going out to eat as a family are occasions that we anticipate on a regular basis. But, there are times when we cannot all be at the same place at the same time, especially since Story entered the scene. We had to consider such factors as weather, stamina, nap times, and attention span when deciding who can attend certain events. Sometimes Ross or I would stay at home with him and other times Ross and I would go and one of the kids would stay at home with him. I cannot recall a time when there's been any hard feelings over staying or going—everyone simply adjusted. The addition of a baby brother has helped to grow a heart of service in our older children unlike I've ever seen in them before. It could have something to do with how he came into the world.

It was early Wednesday morning, the day before Thanksgiving. Outside it was snowing lightly and I decided to go for a walk. Never mind the fact that my due date was two days away. I was determined to gain no more than 25 pounds during this pregnancy and I didn't have much wiggle room left.

At the halfway point of my walk, I felt some twinges in my lower abdomen, but thought *Maybe I'm just pushing myself too hard.* I decided to shorten my walk and head back up the hill to return home. Once I arrived at home and sat down, the twinges continued, only stronger now. *Okay, this is familiar,* I thought smiling to myself. It had been eight years since I last felt contractions and quite honestly, I never thought I would feel them again. At 40 years of age God had put life into my womb and even more miraculously, He had given me peace about it.

I sat for a while in the quiet of a home on holiday break. At 6:30 in the morning, there was not the usual hustle and bustle of a teacher dad and three students getting ready to leave for their school day. There was only silence. I began counting the minutes between contractions and mentally preparing myself for what was ahead. *Breathe in through the nose, pant out through the mouth,* I reminded myself.

After counting the time gap, I realized that my contractions were just under 15 minutes apart. I called the hospital to let them know. "Call us back when they are 10 minutes apart consistently for an hour and don't have anything to eat or drink," they advised me.

I woke Ross up to let him know about what had transpired and the instruction that I'd been given. Then I made what little arrangements that needed to be made in preparation for going to the hospital—phone calls/texts to relatives, instructions for neighbors helping with our kids, adding toiletries to my bag, etc. The contractions continued and after about an hour, began coming regularly 7-10 minutes apart. I let Ross know and called the hospital again. They instructed me to come in.

We arrived at the hospital, were checked in through the ER, and taken up to the obstetrics floor. All the beds in the wing were full so we were put in a holding room to begin paperwork as they monitored my progress. The contractions continued to be about 7 minutes apart. I heard the clinicians talking about the waveforms they were seeing on the monitor while tracking my contractions. There seemed to be no sense of urgency. Thinking that delivery time was close, I let the staff know that I wanted an epidural. They assured me that they would meet my request, but I hadn't even gotten an IV placed yet.

Close to an hour had passed without anyone coming to check in. Thirsty from not having anything to drink since early that morning, I requested some water. A nurse came in with one of the clinicians. When they entered, I was on my hands and knees breathing through a contraction. The clinician waited for it to pass then spoke, "Your contractions have not progressed to the point of bringing about a delivery. We are going to discharge you to labor at home. When your contractions are closer together, call us to come in."

My mind was clamoring. I had come prepared to have a baby and was being sent home. I didn't know how to respond, so I just said, "Okay."

As Ross and I walked back down the same corridors that I had been wheeled through hours earlier, I had to stop periodically as a contraction gripped my midsection. "Are you sure you don't want to just hang out in the hospital instead of going home?" he asked. "It doesn't seem like it's worth leaving just to come right back in a couple of hours." We lived about a half hour away and the light snow had turned into a heavy snow that covered trees and walkways visible through the breezeway windows. "No," I responded, "let's just come back later like they said."

Contractions continued for the duration of our ride home. Once we got home, Ross took a nap on the couch while I sat on the floor and had a bowl of cereal. After eating, the squeezing came on me with a vengeance. I wasn't even timing it anymore I was just trying to make it through each one and then ramp up mentally for the one that was coming down the line. Suddenly I felt the urge to go to the bathroom. I made it there, breathless from the mammoth grip around my waist. I didn't know which end to put on the toilet bowl—my head or my bottom. The latter won out and after going I sank to the floor in exhaustion. I thought to myself, *I have to be close to delivery now. I gotta call Ross to help me up.* No sooner did the thought leave my brain when a massive contraction overcame me and gushed amniotic fluid all over the bathroom floor.

"*Ross!*" I bellowed. Hearing the primal tone to my voice Ross appeared immediately in the doorway. "My water broke," I strained under the pain of the contractions coming now one on top of the other. "Okay, let's get you some new clothes and get to the hospital." He instructed the boys, who were very aware of the situation after hearing me scream, to get Mommy some clothes and clean up my mess.

I could barely move. I tried to get up off the floor, to take my pants off, but it just wasn't working. Ross tried to help me, but I was like a wet noodle—the contractions held me captive.

"I have to get to the bathtub," I panted to him. I started crawling out of the first-floor bathroom making my way towards the stairs. "No," Ross retorted sternly trying to keep his cool. "We need to get to the hospital. If you would just let me help you, we could be there in no time." After having slept through much of my labor, he didn't realize how close my contractions were. "The baby is coming NOW!" I yelled beginning my ascent up the stairs. At this point it hit him. "What do I do?" he asked nervously. "Call Deb," I breathed out trying not to bear down. Deb is a good friend and neighbor up the street who is a registered nurse. We've called upon her in the past for help, especially when I have been unable to be mommy and nurse at the same time. This was one of those times.

Knowing that the baby was going to arrive in our house in moments, I was so relieved to hear my husband's curt conversation with Deb. Praise God she is home! That was blessing number one. She could have been out shopping, off visiting relatives, or plain just not have answered the phone. But God saw to it that she was available to me. As I write this, I am tearing up over God's amazing grace.

By the end of the phone call, I had reached the top of the steps and could go no further. The pressure was unbelievable. "The baby's coming!" I screamed. Morgan and Blaise were holed up in the boys' room which was right across from where I lay sprawled out on the floor. Morgan, previously napping, was wide awake now. Hunter was downstairs on post waiting for our neighbor while calling 911. Ross hurried to my side. "I have to get my pants off." He promptly helped me although I'm certain he wished I were making that statement under different circumstances. With my pants off and Ross in position to see all the action, he said almost as if he were cursing, "Oh my gosh there's the head!" I was terrified. I had no control over what was happening inside my body.

Just then Deb whisked in through the door and up the stairs with a partner—her daughter Caitlyn. Caitlyn, an ER nurse, just happened to be visiting the day before Thanksgiving. I don't dare call this luck. It is an illustration of the provision of a mighty God who cares for me and for you.

At this crucial point when the baby was crowning, Deb stepped in and relieved Ross in more ways than one. Caitlyn sat by my head and helped me to stay calm while asking Ross to retrieve necessary items for delivery. Before I knew it, I was being asked to push. No problem—I was ready. I pushed once. I pushed again. "Oh, it's a boy!" my neighbor exclaimed likely amused by seeing boy parts after having three girls herself. "Thank you, Lord," I cried like a baby as the events of the last several hours whirled around in my head.

Eventually the ambulance arrived on the scene and worked together with our neighbors to care for Story and me. They were so gracious and patient. As much as there was an urgent need to get us to the hospital for evaluation and delivery of the placenta (which incidentally came a lot slower than the baby), the team was very patient. They worked diligently, but also lovingly. Much of the time while they attended to me, Story was with Ross and the kids downstairs wrapped in a towel getting to know his new family.

What a priceless opportunity! Our kids got to experience the miracle and contribute to their sibling being born. Certainly, we were blessed by neighbors that readily came to our aid. But I cannot neglect mentioning how much our kids did to help us and their baby brother. Individually or in some combined form they cleaned up the bathroom floor, called loved ones with the news, got the baby things to keep warm, and remained calm throughout the entire ordeal.

Upon determining that the baby and I were stabilized, the EMTs got us strapped into a stretcher and carried us out to the ambulance. At this point I lost it. "This wasn't how it was supposed to be!" I remember blubbering. The thought of heading back to the very hospital that had sent me home when I needed help left me feeling vulnerable. Deb came to my side to console me and remind me that God had taken care of us. He already knew how this baby boy would come into the world. It was only a surprise to everybody else.

An additional surprise was that this baby was not a girl. As I shared in Chapter 1, we didn't have plans for housing a boy because our three-bedroom home already had two boys in one room, our daughter in her own room, and Ross and me in the remaining room. So, although we had picked a name for a girl, we hadn't determined a name for our son. When Ross left the hospital the first night, he requested that we both come up with a list of names to discuss in the morning. Later that night I made my list. When he arrived the next morning, he showed me his with about 15 names. I showed him mine with only one name—Story William Webb. He gave me a sideways glance as if to say, "Really?" We had considered the name Story as a middle name for a girl, but never as a first name and certainly not for a boy. But then I explained.

"Whenever we share with people about how he came into the world, the common response has been, 'What an awesome story!' His birth is a testimony of God's protection and provision in his life. People will ask us, and one day ask him, how he got his name and we will have the opportunity to share about God's goodness." He relaxed at hearing this and seemed to be with me.

I continued, "As for the middle name, William is your middle name and it's Deb and Caitlyn's last name—in honor of the three people who helped to deliver him." By the look on his face I could tell I had dropped the mic.

And so, it was settled. Story William Webb.

This child has brought an amazing dynamic of selflessness to our family, especially the among the kids. They've readily pitched in with his care—even during the diaper stage. Because of them, Ross and I can go out for an evening knowing that he is in the hands of responsible siblings who love and care for him. I can recall occasions when my oldest son would tote Story's 35-pound body to and from the vehicle, not to mention strapping him into his cumbersome car seat. From day one Morgan and Blaise have each willingly entertained him when I'm busy with other responsibilities. As they routinely sacrifice to serve their little brother, they actively demonstrate Jesus' heart to a watching world.

Being a family of Christ followers, we know that we are in the spotlight. We stand out because we don't do things like the world does. We act differently. At school banquets, our kids' parties, and in restaurants, we pray before we eat, just like at home.

As a teacher and coach, my husband doesn't use profanity and doesn't tolerate it from the students. We drink water and soda instead of alcohol at social events. Ross and I participate in opportunities that help us to grow closer to Jesus and we encourage the same in our children.

Do we mess up? Absolutely. Do people see us mess up? I hope so. If not, they may mistake being a Christian as some type of club to which they cannot gain membership, when, in reality, failure makes you a prime candidate.

I heard a speaker talk once about having a family brand. The way he explained it was it is not so much about what you do, like: "The Linnenbachs are beach people" or "The Davis' volunteer at the animal shelter." A family brand is about who you are. What is at the core of your family's structure? That's a family brand.

Many families I know have athletics as their core. Just as marketing decisions are made based on branding, an athletics schedule will determine what's in this family's best interest. Other families may have money (too much or lack of) as their core. Therefore, decisions for this family revolve around finances. The list can go on and on. The interesting thing is that most families have a "brand" and don't even know it. Simply put, what manifests on the outside is based on what is important on the inside.

People outside of our church know that the Webbs are a Godly family. Other labels I have heard are "spiritual," "religious," "saintly." The bottom line is we have made it clear that we put God first. How? Someone shares a concern with us and we offer to pray with them. Ross and I greet one another with a kiss whenever we see one another or leave one another. Our family says, "I forgive you" to another person after receiving an apology for an offense. Ross and I do not habitually talk negatively about each other in front of others. God's Word and not peer expectations direct our actions.

We use the same language in front of adults that we use in front of children. When people come over to our house, we pray before a meal with them. In regard to all of this, I could say, it's just what we do. But it's more than that. We do it because we gave our lives over to Jesus Christ and live for Him.

Following are some specific examples of how we have lived out our Christianity among our children's peers. As our daughter Morgan grew older, she began asking to go to more social gatherings. We can trust her with such a privilege because of our relationship with her and our knowledge of her friends. Once she asked about going over to a friend's house who was home without a parent. This friend just happened to be a male but male or female the answer is no. The friend lived close by and I offered for her to invite him over to our house. That's just what she did. Not only does this ensure accountability for them both, but it gives us the opportunity to demonstrate Jesus' love as a family.

What did I do? I opened the door and greeted him. I offered him a drink while Morgan made lunch. I got his phone back for him from her little brother when he refused to hand it over. Little things that made him feel welcomed and comfortable. As parents, we can be scary to our kids' friends. When I was a kid, some of my friends' parents always made me feel like they wanted me to be at their home. Others not so much. I hope to be the former rather than the latter. The young man who visited also saw a framed article we have hanging in our living room that tells the story of me being a living kidney donor. This seemed to affect him deeply as he came to me and asked me about it. There was no need for me to preach to him. He saw my life lived out through a visit to our home.

Our oldest son Hunter had a one-year stint on the wrestling team and, on some occasions, needed us to pick him up from practice or meets. Mid-season he started this habit of having a buddy with him who also needed a ride home. First it was regularly a young man in our neighborhood. Then it got to the point where it seemed to be a new face every time. After laying down some ground rules (i.e. call us first to ask if we are available to give someone a ride home rather than walking down to the car with the friend and asking us with the friend right there), it became a joy to provide the young men with this service. We got to know some kids that we wouldn't have normally interacted with and they got to know us. Oftentimes they got to know at least one of Hunter's other siblings as well because I usually had someone in the vehicle with me. The simple act of serving someone can show love and begin relationships. That's what Jesus did.

CONCLUSION

So, what happened with our son Hunter's post-high school plans? (See Chapter 3.) After some time, he started warming up to conversations about college. First, a conversation with a teacher got him thinking about how a college peer group would be beneficial to his future vocation. Later, as a high school senior, he was accepting of looking into taking college classes focused on his future vocation. Then during orientation for these classes, he had the opportunity to connect with a college student majoring in his area of interest. Following this encounter, he made the decision to attend community college.

Will it always work out the way that we as parents want it to work out? No, it will not. And because we are not God, it should not. But I know that it will work out for good. Romans 8:28 promises us this. It says,

And we know that in all things God works for the good of those who love him, who have been called according to his purpose.

Be mindful however that "for the good" in God's eyes may not look good in our eyes. We don't see like He sees. We don't think like He thinks. And we certainly don't know like He knows. Even with our own children.

I offer myself as an example. I was molested as a child. When I was a baby, just delivered, newborn cry filling the room and my parents' hearts, do you think they would ever have considered sexual abuse with the good things God would allow in my future? Certainly not. Maybe they thought about my first steps, first words, first day of school, the day I got married. But I don't believe such a horrid thought even crossed their minds. How could *that* be "good"? Well I wouldn't say it was good either. I would say it was part of "all things." It's something that happened. It's something that hurt. It's also something that helped me to know God. And in knowing God, all kinds of wounds inside of me have been, are being, and will be healed.

So, when I think about my kids and what they might go through because of their own or someone else's poor choices, I am able to think about how God has so mercifully provided "the good" through "all things" in my life. I am not some poor soul who went through hell and is to be pitied. No, I am a sinner whose sins are equal to that of the one who violated me so many years ago. I am a human saved by the blood of Jesus Christ who came to this Earth for the purpose of giving me and you relationship with God our Father. For this reason, I have freedom to parent, to mess up, to be forgiven, and to receive God's grace to try again.

How fortunate we are to be given such a responsibility for raising His children! As we come to realize to Whom they belong, we can truly hand over the reins while we parent through the seasons.

EXTRA!!! EXTRA!!!

I hope you like leftovers! Just like in a movie, some of the original content has to be left on the cutting room floor. Please enjoy these extra helpings of parenting wisdom.

FIRST COMES LOVE (CHAPTER 1)

Ultimately, Jesus is to be our first love. Show your kids how He takes priority over your relationship with them and makes it even better.

TRANSITIONING (CHAPTER 3)

Bedtime Practices

Our three oldest children (16, 14, and 10 at the time of this writing) have staggered bedtimes. We started this practice about three years prior. I had viewed a series about raising children and differences in siblings based on personality as well as birth order. One of the topics it mentioned was how younger siblings are born into community and don't really know anything other than having at least one other kid around. The oldest sibling however had a season where it was just them and their parents. Not only did they have a taste of being at the center of life, but they also have some rights as the firstborn. Certainly nothing can be done about having another sibling—they are here to stay. But parents can give the firstborn some privileges in recognition of their status. One of these privileges is a later bedtime than their sibling(s).

When firstborns get a later bedtime, it sends a message. Whether little brother or sister acknowledge it or not, their older sibling is special. As parents, we tend to send the opposite message. Younger siblings get a sense that the world revolves around them. After all, they are so cute (everybody tells them so), and they get attention for everything that they do (good and bad). But when bedtime rolls around, they see that there's a new sheriff in town as their sweet little buns get tucked into bed and Big Sister is still up watching her favorite television show. Especially in families where younger siblings have stronger personalities than their bigs, this is a simple practice that declares the littles' place in the family line-up.

Additionally, older siblings have waking hours without the young ones around. This is an experience that they had a taste of, however long or short it was, prior to the arrival of another child. Time alone or time alone with parents is not as accessible as it was previously. A later bedtime allows for this opportunity and can fill the need for personal time or interaction with mom and dad.

It was difficult beginning this practice at first. With three kids at the time, we had purposed to put them all in bed at the same time so that we could have time alone together as a couple. However, we felt that the shift in our family dynamics would far outweigh the cost of our sacrifice. In particular, the 10-year old was and remains very strong-willed and his brother, five years his senior, is very laid back. We recognized that giving Hunter this bedtime privilege would send a message to Blaise about his brother's position in relation to himself. That message is ...

You and Hunter are not equals. He is older than you and his seniority alone is to be respected.

Selfish Sidebar

As I wrote about our children becoming independent in making their lunches, God led me to share the following about my marriage…

The only person whose lunch I packed in our house was Ross. He does it now, but at the time I did this so he would have one less thing to do when he is preparing to leave for his workday. When he initially asked me to do this several years ago, I remember thinking, *I just got all the kids trained to make their own lunch and now I have to make lunch for a capable adult?* But then God calmed me down and reminded me of the verse I shared with you in Chapter 2.

Do nothing out of selfish ambition or vain conceit, but in humility consider others better than yourselves. Each of you should look not only to your own interests, but also to the interests of others. (Philippians 2:3-4)

It was clear that I was being selfish and that by making Ross's lunch I could live out this verse by seeing to his interests. Eventually, God has changed my selfish attitude in this area and helped me to see how my husband is blessed through my service.

STOP IT RIGHT NOW BEFORE YOU GET YOUR BEATS BUTT! (CHAPTER 5)

A logical consequence we use with our children for using "potty language," as we call it, is putting a bar of soap in their mouths. Currently we are using one of the soaps we kept from a hotel stay. Although the soap tastes bad either way, you're lucky if you're the first one to have it in your mouth. Why? Because the same bar is used for every offender until it is worn out or too broken up. Therefore, an already negative consequence is amplified by sucking on a previously sucked on bar of soap. Very effective.

BE A FAN (CHAPTER 6)

One final note on this topic of extracurriculars—raffles. Most groups use them in some shape or form to raise funds for the expenses that go with extra activities. Ross and I have made the decision not to participate in raffles. To be honest, we've slipped a few times (I can probably count on one hand the number of times we have slipped), but we don't make a practice of buying raffle tickets of any kind. We look at raffles as a form of gambling. And realistically we don't have money to gamble. If we're buying something, we budget it. But to put money into a chance, well, it's gambling. Not worth it to us and not a good use of the income with which God has blessed us.

We'll buy overpriced chocolates, subs, school spirit wear, and even frozen desserts—if they are budgeted. But we don't do the raffle thing. When it is a requirement, we do something called a "buyout" which is when you pay a set price to make up for whatever tickets you didn't sell or buy for an opportunity at a chance to win. It's often more expensive to do, but for us compromising this principle is even more costly.

I SCREEN, YOU SCREEN, WE ALL SCREEN (CHAPTER 7)

A wonderful resource to help with developing digital device disciplines is Catherine Price's *How to Break Up with Your Phone*.[1] In it you'll find practical, temporary, and permanent changes you can implement to help break the control your phone has over you. I provided it to our son Hunter as required reading when he was unable to set boundaries on his own. He began applying the author's suggestions and eventually overcame some significant hurdles relating to his device use. Most tips are ones that can be implemented immediately without expense. I encourage you to check out this resource not only for helping your child, but for helping yourself as well.

---

1 Catherine Price, *How to Break Up with Your Phone: The 30-Day Plan to Take Back Your Life*, Ten Speed Press, 2018.

www.ingramcontent.com/pod-product-compliance
Lightning Source LLC
Chambersburg PA
CBHW060435090426
42733CB00011B/2288